GOODSON MUMBA

Building Better Communites

Handbook on Public Policy

First edition

ISBN: 9798336054378

This book was professionally typeset on Reedsy.
Find out more at reedsy.com

Contents

Preface

In a world where the complexities of governance and societal needs are ever-evolving, the role of public policy has never been more crucial. "Building Better Communities: Handbook on Public Policy" is a comprehensive guide designed to empower policymakers, community leaders, and engaged citizens with the knowledge and tools necessary to navigate the challenges and opportunities of modern governance.

The inspiration for this book stems from a vision to bridge the gap between theoretical concepts and practical applications in the realm of public policy. It is my firm belief that strong, resilient communities are built on the foundation of well-informed policies that address the diverse needs of the population while promoting equity, sustainability, and innovation.

From the bustling streets of Lusaka to the serene villages of Kasama, the impact of well-crafted policies on education, healthcare, economic development, and social justice is profound. This handbook aims to capture those experiences and translate them into actionable insights that can be applied across various contexts.

Each chapter of this book delves into a critical aspect of public policy, providing both a theoretical framework and practical examples. We begin with an introduction to the fundamental concepts and historical development of public policy, setting the stage for a deeper exploration of specific policy areas such as economic development, social equity, infrastructure, and environmental sustainability. Throughout the book, real-world case studies and dramatized narratives bring the concepts to life, illustrating the dynamic interplay between policy decisions and community outcomes.

The book also addresses the contemporary challenges facing policymakers, including political polarization, technological disruptions, and global health pandemics. These sections underscore the importance of adaptability, collaboration, and ethical considerations in policy-making processes. By examining these issues through a global lens, with a particular focus on the Zambian context, we aim to provide a holistic understanding of the interconnected nature of public policy.

"Building Better Communities" is not merely a handbook; it is a call to action. It urges readers to actively participate in the policy-making process, to advocate for inclusive and sustainable policies, and to engage in constructive dialogue with diverse stakeholders. It is my hope that this book will serve as a valuable resource for current and future policymakers, equipping them with the insights and strategies needed to build stronger, more resilient communities.

I extend my deepest gratitude to the numerous individuals and communities who have contributed their experiences and wisdom to this book. Your stories and insights have enriched this work and will undoubtedly inspire many more to join the collective effort of building better communities.

With great optimism for the future,
Goodson Mumba

Acknowledgments

I would like to eternally and gratefully acknowledge the Almighty God for the infinite intelligence from His universal mind where we draw from all that we come to know and are yet to know. May I also acknowledge and thank everyone that has played a part in my journey of life in terms of spiritual, moral, emotional and material support.

Dedication

I extend my sincerest gratitude to my beloved wife, Edith Mumba, and our children, Angelina, Lubuto, Letticia, Lulumbi, and Butusho, for their unwavering support and understanding throughout the conception, writing, and eventual publication of this book, despite the sacrifices and challenges they endured.

Disclaimer

This book is a work of fiction. Names, characters, businesses, places, events, and incidents are either the products of the author's imagination or used in a fictitious manner. Any resemblance to actual persons, living or dead, or actual events is purely coincidental.

1

Chapter 1: Introduction to Public Policy

Understanding the Role of Public Policy

"The Call to Serve"

In the rural village of Kasama, Zambia, the sun rose over the rolling hills, casting a golden glow upon the thatched roofs and bustling streets below. Among the villagers, a sense of anticipation hung in the air as they gathered for a community meeting in the central square.

At the forefront of the crowd stood Chilufya, a young man with a fire in his eyes and a determination in his heart. As the meeting began, the village elders spoke of the challenges facing their community: access to clean water, healthcare, and education. The murmurs of concern rippled through the crowd, but Chilufya remained steadfast, his mind racing with ideas.

Later that evening, Chilufya retreated to the modest home

he shared with his family, his thoughts consumed by the plight of his fellow villagers. As he sat by the flickering light of a kerosene lamp, he reached for a worn copy of the "Building Better Communities" handbook that he had received upon completing his studies.

As Chilufya flipped through the pages of the handbook, he came across a chapter titled "Understanding the Role of Public Policy." Intrigued, he delved into its contents, absorbing every word with rapt attention.

The chapter explained that public policy was more than just a set of rules and regulations—it was the guiding force behind the decisions made by governments to address societal issues and improve the lives of citizens. It emphasized the importance of identifying problems, evaluating potential solutions, and implementing policies that would have a meaningful impact on communities.

As Chilufya read on, he realized that he held the key to unlocking change within his own village. Armed with knowledge and a newfound sense of purpose, he vowed to become a champion for his community, using the principles of public policy to guide his efforts.

With the first light of dawn, Chilufya emerged from his home, his resolve stronger than ever. As he set out to mobilize his fellow villagers and chart a course for the future, he knew that the journey ahead would be challenging, but he was determined to make a difference—one policy at a time.

Historical Overview of Public Policy Development

"Echoes of the Past"

As the days turned into weeks, Chilufya's determination to enact change in his village only grew stronger. Guided by the principles outlined in the "Building Better Communities" handbook, he embarked on a journey to explore the historical roots of public policy development, seeking inspiration from the lessons of the past

Chilufya sought out the wisdom of the village elders, gathering around the communal fire as they shared stories passed down through generations. They spoke of a time when their ancestors had come together to address common challenges, devising communal solutions that ensured the well-being of all.

Intrigued by these tales, Chilufya delved deeper into the history of public policy, studying the ancient traditions and customs that had shaped governance in Zambia for centuries. He learned of the intricate systems of justice and administration that had fostered peace and prosperity among the diverse tribes of the land.

But Chilufya also uncovered darker chapters in Zambia's history, where colonial powers had imposed policies that marginalized indigenous communities and exploited natural resources for their own gain. He listened intently as the elders recounted stories of resistance and resilience, reminding him of the importance of standing up for justice in the face of adversity.

Armed with this newfound knowledge, Chilufya realized that the struggles of the past held valuable lessons for the present. Just as his ancestors had united to overcome challenges, so too would he and his fellow villagers join forces to build a brighter future for generations to come.

With a renewed sense of purpose, Chilufya set out to apply the insights gleaned from history to the present-day issues facing his community. He knew that by honoring the legacy of those who had come before him, he could pave the way for a more equitable and prosperous tomorrow. And so, with the echoes of the past guiding his steps, Chilufya forged ahead, determined to leave a lasting impact on his village and beyond.

Key Concepts and Terminologies in Public Policy

"The Language of Change"

In the quiet hours before dawn, Chilufya sat beneath the sprawling branches of an ancient baobab tree, the pages of the "Building Better Communities" handbook spread out before him. As the first light of day began to filter through the leaves, he turned his attention to the next chapter, eager to delve into the key concepts and terminologies that would guide his journey.

With furrowed brow, Chilufya poured over the pages, absorbing the intricate language of public policy like a scholar deciphering an ancient text. Terms like "policy formulation," "policy implementation," and "policy evaluation" danced across the page, each one holding within it the potential to bring about meaningful change.

As he delved deeper, Chilufya began to grasp the interconnected nature of these concepts, understanding how each stage of the policy process contributed to the larger goal of building better communities. He marveled at the complexity of governance, realizing that effective policy-making required not only vision and passion but also strategic planning and careful consideration of trade-offs.

But amidst the sea of technical jargon, Chilufya also discovered something deeper—a set of values that underpinned the practice of public policy. Concepts like equity, justice, and accountability resonated deeply with him, serving as guiding principles in his quest to create a more just and inclusive society.

Armed with this newfound understanding, Chilufya felt a sense of clarity wash over him. No longer intimidated by the complexities of public policy, he saw them as tools to be wielded in service of his community, each term and concept a stepping stone on the path to progress.

With a renewed sense of purpose, Chilufya closed the handbook, the knowledge contained within it now etched into his mind and heart. As he rose to his feet, ready to face the challenges that lay ahead, he knew that the language of change was his to speak—and with it, he would shape the future of his village and beyond.

Importance of Public Policy in Building Strong Communities

"Foundations of Progress"

As the sun reached its zenith in the cloudless sky, casting a warm glow over the village of Kasama, Chilufya found himself surrounded by a buzz of activity. Farmers tended to their crops, children played in the dusty streets, and elders gathered beneath the shade of a towering mango tree to share stories and wisdom.

Amidst the hustle and bustle of daily life, Chilufya paused to reflect on the importance of public policy in shaping the fabric of their community. He recalled the words from the "Building Better Communities" handbook, which emphasized that effective policies were the bedrock upon which strong, resilient communities were built.

With a sense of clarity, Chilufya began to see the ways in which public policy touched every aspect of village life. From access to clean water and healthcare, to education and economic opportunities, policies played a critical role in determining the quality of life for every resident.

He thought of his own family, and the struggles they faced due to inadequate infrastructure and limited resources. But he also saw the potential for change—the opportunity to leverage the power of public policy to address these challenges and build a brighter future for all.

As he looked around at his fellow villagers, Chilufya felt a surge of determination. He knew that by harnessing the principles of public policy, they could create a community where everyone had the opportunity to thrive. Where no one was left behind, and where the collective well-being of all was prioritized above all else.

With a newfound sense of purpose, Chilufya pledged to become a champion for his community, using the lessons from the handbook to guide his efforts. He knew that the road ahead would be long and challenging, but he also knew that with determination and perseverance, they could lay the foundations of progress upon which their community would flourish for generations to come.

Challenges and Opportunities in Public Policy Making

"Navigating the Terrain"

As the sun dipped below the horizon, casting long shadows across the village of Kasama, Chilufya found himself seated beneath the ancient baobab tree once more, the "Building Better Communities" handbook open before him. With a furrowed brow, he turned his attention to the next section, eager to explore the challenges and opportunities that awaited on the path of public policy making.

With each word he read, Chilufya felt a weight settle in the pit of his stomach. The handbook painted a stark picture of the obstacles that lay ahead—bureaucratic red tape, limited resources, and entrenched interests all threatened to derail their efforts before they even began.

But amidst the challenges, Chilufya also saw glimmers of hope. The handbook spoke of opportunities for innovation and collaboration, of grassroots movements that had sparked real change in communities around the world. It reminded him that while the road ahead would be difficult, it was not insurmountable.

As he pondered the lessons of the handbook, Chilufya thought back to the resilience of his fellow villagers, their unwavering spirit in the face of adversity. He realized that while the challenges of public policy making were daunting, they were not without solutions.

With determination burning in his chest, Chilufya closed the handbook, a plan beginning to take shape in his mind. He knew that they would need to approach their work with creativity and ingenuity, leveraging the strengths of their community to overcome the obstacles in their path.

As he rose to his feet, ready to face the challenges that lay ahead, Chilufya felt a renewed sense of purpose coursing through his veins. With the "Building Better Communities" handbook as their guide, he knew that he and his fellow villagers could navigate the terrain of public policy making, turning challenges into opportunities and forging a brighter future for all.

Ethical Considerations in Public Policy Decision Making

"Guiding Principles"

As the moon rose high in the night sky, casting a soft glow over the village of Kasama, Chilufya sat alone in the stillness, the "Building Better Communities" handbook clasped in his hands. With a sense of reverence, he turned to the final subpoint of Chapter 1, eager to explore the ethical considerations that would shape their journey in public policy decision making.

With each word he read, Chilufya felt a weight settle upon his shoulders. The handbook spoke of the importance of ethical leadership and integrity in governance, reminding him that the decisions they made would have real consequences for the lives of their fellow villagers.

As he reflected on the lessons of the handbook, Chilufya felt a deep sense of responsibility wash over him. He knew that their pursuit of progress must be guided by principles of fairness, justice, and respect for human dignity.

But as he looked out over the sleeping village, Chilufya also saw the challenges that lay ahead. The temptation to prioritize personal gain over the common good, the pressure to compromise their values in the face of opposition—these were the ethical dilemmas that threatened to derail their efforts.

With a heavy heart, Chilufya knew that they would need to remain vigilant, holding fast to their ethical principles even in the face of adversity. He vowed to lead by example, to uphold the trust placed in him by his fellow villagers, and to always strive to do what was right, even when it was difficult.

As he closed the handbook and made his way back to his home, Chilufya felt a sense of resolve settle within him. With the ethical considerations outlined in the handbook as their guiding light, he knew that he and his fellow villagers could navigate the complexities of public policy decision making with integrity and honor, forging a path toward a brighter future for all.

2

Chapter 2: The Policy Making Process

Identifying Policy Issues and Priorities

"The Journey Begins"

In the heart of Kasama, where the red earth met the sprawling savannah, Chilufya stood before a gathering of his fellow villagers, the "Building Better Communities" handbook clutched in his hands. As he addressed the crowd, his voice rang out with passion and purpose, echoing across the dusty streets.

With a sense of urgency, Chilufya spoke of the challenges facing their community—the lack of access to clean water, the scarcity of healthcare facilities, the barriers to education that kept their children from reaching their full potential. He urged his fellow villagers to join him in a quest to identify the key policy issues and priorities that would shape their future.

As the sun dipped below the horizon, the villagers gathered beneath the shade of a towering baobab tree, their faces illuminated by the soft glow of lantern light. Together, they shared their stories and concerns, each voice adding depth to the conversation.

Amidst the discussions, patterns began to emerge—common themes that underscored the interconnected nature of their challenges. They spoke of the need for sustainable solutions that would address the root causes of poverty and inequality, of the importance of investing in infrastructure and social services to uplift the entire community.

With each word spoken, Chilufya felt a sense of clarity wash over him. He knew that by listening to the voices of his fellow villagers, they could uncover the policy issues and priorities that truly mattered to their community. And armed with this knowledge, they could begin the journey towards meaningful change.

As the meeting drew to a close, Chilufya and his fellow villagers formed a pact—a commitment to work together, to prioritize the needs of the most vulnerable among them, and to never lose sight of their shared vision for a brighter future.

With the first light of dawn, Chilufya set out to document their discussions, the words of his fellow villagers echoing in his mind. As he walked through the streets of Kasama, he knew that the journey ahead would be long and challenging. But with the "Building Better Communities" handbook as their guide, he was confident that they could navigate the twists and turns of the policy-making process, one step at a time.

Stakeholder Analysis and Engagement

"Strength in Unity"

As the sun rose over the village of Kasama, Chilufya gathered a diverse group of villagers beneath the sprawling branches of a baobab tree. With the "Building Better Communities" handbook open before him, he began to discuss the next step in their journey towards policy change.

Chilufya emphasized the importance of stakeholder analysis and engagement—a crucial step in their quest to build strong, inclusive policies. He spoke of the need to identify and involve all those who would be affected by their decisions, from local leaders and community organizations to marginalized groups whose voices had long been ignored.

As the villagers listened intently, Chilufya outlined their plan for stakeholder engagement. They would hold community forums and listening sessions, reaching out to people from all walks of life to ensure that every voice was heard. They would also map out the networks of power and influence within their community, identifying key stakeholders who could help advance their cause.

With a sense of purpose, Chilufya and his fellow villagers set out to engage with their community. They traveled from village to village, holding meetings under the shade of trees and in the courtyards of local leaders. They listened as farmers spoke of the challenges they faced in accessing markets for their crops, as mothers voiced their concerns about the lack of healthcare for their children, and as young people shared their dreams of a brighter future.

As they listened, Chilufya and his team began to see the connections between their various stakeholders, recognizing the power that lay in unity. They forged alliances with local leaders, enlisted the support of community organizations, and empowered marginalized groups to speak up and demand change.

With each new voice added to the conversation, Chilufya felt a sense of momentum building—a collective energy that propelled them forward on their journey. He knew that by engaging with their stakeholders in a spirit of openness and collaboration, they could harness the strength of their community to create policies that truly reflected their needs and aspirations.

As the sun dipped below the horizon, Chilufya and his team returned to the village, their hearts full with the knowledge that they were not alone in their quest for change. With the support of their fellow villagers behind them, they knew that anything was possible. And with the "Building Better Communities" handbook lighting their way, they were ready to take the next step on their journey towards a brighter future.

Policy Formulation: Developing Solutions and Alternatives

"Seeds of Innovation"

Underneath the vast expanse of the Zambian sky, Chilufya gathered with his team of dedicated villagers, the "Building Better Communities" handbook resting open on a makeshift table. As they discussed their next steps in the policy-making process, Chilufya's voice rang out with determination.

With a sense of purpose, Chilufya and his team delved into the task of policy formulation. They knew that to address the pressing challenges facing their community, they would need to develop innovative solutions that addressed the root causes of poverty and inequality.

Drawing inspiration from the handbook's guidance, they began to brainstorm alternatives, exploring a range of ideas and approaches. They considered the needs and perspectives of their stakeholders, seeking to develop policies that would be both effective and inclusive.

As they debated and discussed, Chilufya felt a sense of excitement building within him. He could see the seeds of innovation taking root, as his fellow villagers brought their diverse perspectives and experiences to the table.

Together, they developed a comprehensive plan that addressed the key issues facing their community. They proposed initiatives to improve access to clean water, to expand healthcare services, and to invest in education and economic development.

But they also recognized the importance of flexibility and adaptability in their approach. They knew that the needs of their community were ever-evolving, and that their policies would need to evolve with them.

With a sense of pride, Chilufya and his team presented their policy proposals to the wider community. They listened as their fellow villagers offered feedback and suggestions, refining their ideas to better meet the needs of those they served.

As the meeting drew to a close, Chilufya felt a sense of satisfaction wash over him. He knew that the road ahead would be challenging, but he also knew that they had taken the first step towards creating positive change in their community.

With the "Building Better Communities" handbook as their guide, Chilufya and his team were ready to embark on the next phase of their journey, confident in their ability to overcome any obstacle that stood in their way.

Policy Implementation: Turning Ideas into Action

"Turning Vision into Reality"

As the sun cast its warm glow over the village of Kasama, Chilufya and his team stood before their fellow villagers, the "Building Better Communities" handbook held firmly in Chilufya's hands. With determination etched on their faces, they prepared to embark on the next phase of their journey: policy implementation.

With a sense of purpose, Chilufya outlined their plan to turn their policy proposals into tangible actions that would bring about real change in their community. He spoke of the importance of commitment and perseverance, emphasizing that their vision could only be realized through determined effort and collaboration.

With the support of their fellow villagers, Chilufya and his team set to work, mobilizing resources and rallying support for their policy initiatives. They worked tirelessly to secure funding, engage with government officials, and build partnerships with local organizations and businesses.

As they began to implement their policies, Chilufya and his team encountered obstacles and challenges at every turn. Bureaucratic red tape, logistical hurdles, and resistance from vested interests threatened to derail their efforts, but they refused to be deterred.

With unwavering determination, they pressed forward, finding creative solutions to overcome each obstacle they encountered. They worked closely with community members to ensure that their policies were tailored to the specific needs of the people they served, and they remained open to feedback and suggestions along the way.

As the months passed, Chilufya and his team began to see the fruits of their labor. Clean water flowed from newly installed taps, healthcare clinics sprang up in remote villages, and children received access to quality education for the first time.

But they knew that their work was far from over. They continued to monitor and evaluate their policies, adjusting their approach as needed to ensure that they were making a meaningful impact on the lives of their fellow villagers.

As the sun set on another day in Kasama, Chilufya and his team gathered beneath the stars, their hearts full with the knowledge that they were making a difference. With the "Building Better Communities" handbook as their guide, they knew that their journey was far from over, but they were more determined than ever to continue turning their vision into reality, one policy at a time.

Monitoring and Evaluation of Policy Impact

"Tracking Progress"

Under the vast expanse of the African sky, Chilufya and his team gathered once more, the "Building Better Communities" handbook open before them. With the next phase of their journey upon them, they turned their attention to the crucial task of monitoring and evaluating the impact of their policies.

With a sense of purpose, Chilufya spoke of the importance

of tracking progress and assessing the effectiveness of their policies. He emphasized that while their initiatives had begun to yield positive results, they could not afford to become complacent.

Together, they developed a comprehensive plan for monitoring and evaluation, drawing on the principles outlined in the handbook. They established key performance indicators and benchmarks to measure the impact of their policies, ensuring that they remained accountable to their fellow villagers.

As they set out to implement their monitoring and evaluation plan, Chilufya and his team encountered challenges and obstacles. Gathering data proved to be a daunting task, and interpreting the results required careful analysis and interpretation.

But they pressed on, undeterred by the challenges they faced. They conducted surveys, interviews, and focus groups, seeking feedback from community members on the impact of their policies. They analyzed data and statistics, identifying trends and patterns that shed light on the effectiveness of their initiatives.

As the months passed, Chilufya and his team began to see the fruits of their labor. They celebrated successes, such as improved access to clean water and healthcare, and they acknowledged areas where further progress was needed.

But they also remained vigilant, recognizing that their work was far from over. They continued to refine their policies, making adjustments based on the feedback and data they collected. They remained committed to their goal of building better communities, knowing that their efforts would have a lasting impact on the lives of their fellow villagers.

As the sun set on another day in Kasama, Chilufya and his

team gathered beneath the stars, their hearts full with the knowledge that they were making a difference. With the "Building Better Communities" handbook as their guide, they knew that their journey was far from over, but they were more determined than ever to continue tracking progress and ensuring that their policies were making a meaningful impact on the lives of their community members.

Policy Revision and Adaptation

"Adapting to Change"

Under the canopy of a majestic baobab tree, Chilufya and his team gathered once again, the "Building Better Communities" handbook open before them. As they continued their journey of policy-making, they turned their attention to the critical task of policy revision and adaptation.

With a sense of determination, Chilufya spoke of the need to remain flexible and responsive in the face of change. He emphasized that while their policies had begun to yield positive results, they must be willing to adapt and evolve as new challenges emerged.

Together, they reviewed the data and feedback they had collected through their monitoring and evaluation efforts. They analyzed trends and identified areas where their policies were falling short, acknowledging that no plan was perfect and that there was always room for improvement.

As they delved into the process of policy revision, Chilufya and his team encountered resistance and skepticism from some quarters. There were those who were hesitant to change, who feared that revising their policies would be a sign of failure.

But Chilufya remained steadfast in his belief that adaptation was a sign of strength, not weakness. He spoke of the importance of listening to the needs of their community and responding with agility and innovation.

With a renewed sense of purpose, Chilufya and his team set to work revising their policies, incorporating new ideas and strategies that would better meet the needs of their fellow villagers. They consulted with experts and sought input from community members, ensuring that their revisions were grounded in the realities of their community.

As they implemented their revised policies, Chilufya and his team began to see the impact of their efforts. Clean water flowed more freely, healthcare services became more accessible, and educational opportunities expanded for all.

But they knew that their work was far from over. They remained committed to the ongoing process of policy revision and adaptation, knowing that the journey towards building better communities was one that would require constant vigilance and effort.

As the sun set on another day in Kasama, Chilufya and his team gathered beneath the baobab tree, their hearts full with the knowledge that they were making a difference. With the "Building Better Communities" handbook as their guide, they knew that they were prepared to face whatever challenges lay ahead, confident in their ability to adapt and evolve in pursuit of their shared vision of a brighter future for all.

3

Chapter 3: Governance Structures and Institutions

Role of Government in Policy Making

"Building Blocks of Governance"

In the heart of Kasama, where the rhythms of village life echoed through the dusty streets, Chilufya and his team gathered once more, the "Building Better Communities" handbook open before them. As they delved into the complexities of governance structures and institutions, they sought to understand the role of government in shaping policy.

With a solemn reverence, Chilufya spoke of the pivotal role that government played in the policy-making process. He emphasized that while their community-driven efforts were essential, they must also work hand-in-hand with government institutions to enact lasting change.

As they discussed the intricacies of governance, Chilufya

and his team began to unravel the web of institutions that governed their lives. They learned of the legislative branch, responsible for passing laws and regulations; the executive branch, charged with implementing policies; and the judicial branch, tasked with upholding the rule of law.

But Chilufya also spoke of the importance of local government in shaping policy at the grassroots level. He emphasized that while national-level institutions played a crucial role, it was often the local councils and authorities that had the most direct impact on the lives of their fellow villagers.

With a sense of empowerment, Chilufya and his team set out to engage with government officials at all levels. They attended council meetings, participated in policy forums, and advocated for their community's needs with passion and determination.

As they navigated the complexities of government bureaucracy, Chilufya and his team encountered challenges and obstacles. They faced skepticism from some officials, who were hesitant to embrace change, and bureaucratic red tape that threatened to stifle their efforts.

But they remained undeterred, knowing that their cause was just and their determination unwavering. They continued to build relationships with government officials, demonstrating the importance of community-driven solutions and the power of partnership in creating lasting change.

As the sun dipped below the horizon, Chilufya and his team gathered beneath the stars, their hearts full with the knowledge that they were not alone in their quest for a better future. With the "Building Better Communities" handbook as their guide, they were prepared to work hand-in-hand with government institutions to shape policies that would improve the lives of their fellow villagers and lay the foundation for a brighter tomorrow.

Legislative Processes and Decision Making

"The Halls of Power"

In the bustling village of Kasama, where the pulse of community life thrummed through the air, Chilufya and his team gathered in a humble meeting hall. The "Building Better Communities" handbook lay open on the table, guiding them through the intricate world of legislative processes and decision making.

Chilufya began by explaining the vital role that legislative processes played in transforming ideas into enforceable policies. He emphasized that understanding how laws were made and decisions were reached was crucial for anyone looking to enact change through official channels.

With a clear sense of purpose, Chilufya and his team decided to travel to the provincial capital to witness the legislative process firsthand. They boarded a rickety bus at dawn, the road winding through the lush Zambian countryside. As they approached the city, the sight of the grand legislative building filled them with a mix of awe and determination.

Inside the legislative chamber, they observed as representatives debated and discussed proposed bills. The air was thick with the energy of democracy in action, each voice contributing to the collective decision-making process. Chilufya watched intently as motions were introduced, amended, and voted upon, the complex dance of governance unfolding before his eyes.

During a break in the session, Chilufya approached one of the local representatives, a woman named Mwamba who had earned a reputation for championing community issues. With respect, he introduced himself and shared the story of Kasama's struggles and aspirations.

Mwamba listened with keen interest, her eyes reflecting the shared passion for community betterment. She explained how legislative processes worked, detailing the stages a bill must pass through—from committee reviews to public hearings and, finally, to a vote on the floor.

Inspired by this conversation, Chilufya and his team began to draft their own policy proposal, focusing on improving access to clean water and healthcare in their village. They outlined the problems, proposed solutions, and gathered data to support their case. With Mwamba's guidance, they learned how to frame their arguments in a way that resonated with legislators and aligned with broader provincial goals.

Back in Kasama, Chilufya and his team held community meetings to gather support and refine their proposal further. They knew that grassroots backing was essential for their initiative to succeed in the legislative arena. Villagers signed petitions, shared their personal stories, and prepared to advocate for the policy at upcoming public hearings.

As the months passed, Chilufya and his team navigated the legislative maze, attending committee meetings and engaging with other representatives. Their persistence paid off as their proposal gained traction, receiving amendments and support from various stakeholders.

On a momentous day, Chilufya stood in the legislative chamber, watching as the vote was called. The room fell silent, and then the decision was announced—the bill had passed. Cheers erupted among the supporters, and tears of joy streamed down the faces of many who had worked tirelessly for this moment.

Returning to Kasama, Chilufya and his team were greeted as heroes. The successful passage of their policy marked the beginning of a new chapter for their village. With the "Building Better Communities" handbook as their constant guide, they had not only navigated the legislative process but also ignited a spirit of hope and empowerment that would continue to drive their community forward.

Under the star-lit sky, Chilufya reflected on their journey. He knew that the road to sustainable change was long and winding, but with determination, unity, and an unwavering commitment to their shared vision, they had proven that even the smallest voices could echo powerfully through the halls of power.

Executive Branch and Administrative Agencies

"Executing the Vision"

The morning sun cast a golden hue over the village of Kasama as Chilufya and his team gathered once more under the familiar baobab tree. With the "Building Better Communities" handbook in hand, they prepared to delve into the next chapter of their journey: understanding the role of the executive branch and administrative agencies in policy implementation.

Chilufya began by explaining the pivotal role that the executive branch and administrative agencies played in turning legislative decisions into practical actions. He emphasized that while passing a bill was a significant achievement, it was only the beginning. The real challenge lay in the effective implementation of those policies.

Determined to learn more, Chilufya and his team decided to visit the provincial capital once again, this time to engage with the executive branch and various administrative agencies responsible for enacting the policies they had fought so hard to see passed.

Upon arriving at the government complex, they were greeted by Mr. Banda, a seasoned civil servant who had spent years navigating the intricacies of policy implementation. Mr. Banda welcomed them warmly and offered to guide them through the labyrinthine world of government administration.

Their first stop was the Department of Health, where they met with Dr. Nkandu, the head of the agency. Dr. Nkandu explained how her department was tasked with translating healthcare policies into actionable programs and services. She spoke of the challenges they faced, from budget constraints to logistical hurdles, and the strategies they employed to overcome them.

Chilufya and his team listened intently as Dr. Nkandu detailed the process of allocating resources, training healthcare workers, and setting up new clinics. They learned about the importance of inter-agency collaboration and the role of data and feedback in refining their approach.

Next, they visited the Department of Water Resources, where Mr. Phiri, the director, explained how his agency was responsible for implementing policies related to water access and sanitation. He showed them maps and blueprints of planned water infrastructure projects, discussing the steps involved in site selection, community engagement, and construction.

Chilufya and his team were struck by the complexity of the implementation process and the dedication of the civil servants who worked tirelessly to bring policies to life. They realized that successful policy implementation required not just vision and planning, but also coordination, perseverance, and a deep understanding of the local context.

Inspired by their visit, Chilufya and his team returned to Kasama with a renewed sense of purpose. They knew that to ensure the success of their policies, they needed to work closely with the executive branch and administrative agencies. They organized meetings with local government officials, shared their experiences, and sought to build strong partnerships.

Together with the local administrators, they developed detailed action plans for their initiatives, ensuring that every step was carefully planned and resourced. They held community workshops to explain the implementation process, encouraging villagers to participate and take ownership of the projects.

As the months went by, the fruits of their labor began to materialize. New healthcare clinics were established, providing much-needed medical services to remote areas. Clean water systems were installed, bringing safe drinking water to every household. The villagers of Kasama felt a tangible improvement in their quality of life, and their trust in the local government grew stronger.

Under the shade of the baobab tree, Chilufya and his team reflected on their journey. They had learned that effective governance required more than just passing laws; it required a concerted effort to translate those laws into real-world actions that improved people's lives.

With the "Building Better Communities" handbook as their guide, they had navigated the complexities of the executive branch and administrative agencies, ensuring that their vision for a better future became a reality. And as they looked ahead, they knew that their work was far from over. But with unity, perseverance, and a steadfast commitment to their community, they were ready to face whatever challenges lay ahead.

Judicial Review and Policy Enforcement

"Justice in Action"

The village of Kasama buzzed with activity as Chilufya and his team gathered under the baobab tree, the "Building Better Communities" handbook open before them. They were about to embark on the next step of their journey, delving into the critical role of judicial review and policy enforcement in the governance process.

Chilufya began by explaining the importance of the judiciary in ensuring that policies were not only implemented effectively but also upheld the principles of justice and fairness. He emphasized that judicial review was a mechanism to check the power of the executive and legislative branches, ensuring that laws and policies adhered to the constitution and protected citizens' rights.

With a renewed sense of purpose, Chilufya and his team decided to visit the provincial courthouse to witness the judicial process firsthand and understand how it influenced policy enforcement. The journey to the courthouse took them through the heart of the provincial capital, where the imposing building stood as a symbol of justice and the rule of law.

Inside the courthouse, they were greeted by Judge Chisanga, a respected jurist known for her commitment to upholding the law. Judge Chisanga welcomed them warmly and offered to explain the judiciary's role in policy enforcement.

As they sat in her chambers, Judge Chisanga spoke about the concept of judicial review. She explained how the courts had the authority to examine the actions of the executive and legislative branches, ensuring that policies and laws complied with the constitution. She emphasized that this oversight was crucial for protecting citizens' rights and maintaining the balance of power within the government.

Judge Chisanga invited them to observe a case in the courtroom—a case that involved a dispute over the implementation of a new healthcare policy. The plaintiffs argued that the policy had been unfairly applied, denying them access to essential medical services. As the case unfolded, Chilufya and his team saw how the judiciary played a vital role in interpreting laws and resolving conflicts.

The judge listened attentively to both sides, weighed the evidence, and delivered a ruling that emphasized fairness and equity. The court ordered a review of the policy's implementation, ensuring that it would be applied justly and without discrimination. This decision reinforced the principle that policies must be enforced in a manner that respected the rights and dignity of all citizens.

Inspired by what they had witnessed, Chilufya and his team returned to Kasama with a deeper understanding of the judiciary's role in governance. They realized that for their policies to be effective and just, they must be prepared to engage with the judicial system, ensuring that their initiatives were legally sound and upheld the rights of their fellow villagers.

Back in the village, they organized workshops to educate the community about their legal rights and the importance of judicial oversight. They encouraged villagers to speak up if they felt that policies were being applied unfairly and assured them that the courts were there to protect their rights.

As the months passed, Chilufya and his team continued to implement their policies, always mindful of the need for transparency and accountability. They worked closely with local legal experts to ensure that their initiatives complied with the law and could withstand judicial scrutiny.

Under the baobab tree, Chilufya and his team reflected on their journey. They had learned that true governance required not only the creation and implementation of policies but also a steadfast commitment to justice and fairness. With the "Building Better Communities" handbook as their guide, they were confident that they could navigate the challenges ahead, ensuring that their vision for a better future was realized through the principles of law and equity.

And as the sun set on another day in Kasama, they knew that their work was far from over. But with unity, determination, and an unwavering commitment to justice, they were ready to face whatever challenges lay ahead, confident in their ability to build a brighter, fairer future for all.

Multi-level Governance: Republican State, and Local Dynamics

"Unity in Diversity"

As dawn broke over the village of Kasama, Chilufya and his team gathered once more under the ancient baobab tree, the "Building Better Communities" handbook open and ready to guide them. Today, they would explore the intricate web of multi-level governance, focusing on the interplay between the republican state and local dynamics.

Chilufya began by explaining the concept of multi-level governance, highlighting the importance of understanding how different levels of government—from national to local—worked together to shape policy and address community needs. He emphasized that effective governance required coordination and collaboration across all levels, each with its unique responsibilities and strengths.

Determined to grasp the full scope of this complex system, Chilufya and his team planned visits to both the national capital, Lusaka, and the provincial capital. They aimed to learn firsthand how policies crafted at the highest levels were implemented locally and how local dynamics influenced national decisions.

Their journey to Lusaka was an eye-opener. The grandeur of the national parliament building stood in stark contrast to the humble surroundings of Kasama. Inside, they met with national legislators and policymakers, including Mr. Zulu, a senior advisor in the Ministry of Local Government. Mr. Zulu welcomed them with enthusiasm, eager to share insights about the republican state's role in governance.

Mr. Zulu explained how national policies were designed to address broad issues affecting the entire country, such as economic development, national security, and public health.

He emphasized that while the national government provided the overarching framework, it was up to local governments to adapt and implement these policies to meet the specific needs of their communities.

Intrigued by this explanation, Chilufya asked about the challenges of ensuring that national policies were effectively implemented at the local level. Mr. Zulu acknowledged that while the intentions behind national policies were often noble, their success depended heavily on local capacity and engagement. He highlighted the importance of strong communication channels and partnerships between different levels of government.

Armed with this new understanding, Chilufya and his team returned to the provincial capital, where they met with Mrs. Mwila, the head of the Provincial Development Office. Mrs. Mwila illustrated how provincial authorities acted as a bridge between the national government and local communities, ensuring that national policies were tailored to regional realities.

She described the collaborative process of policy adaptation, where provincial offices worked with local councils to identify community-specific needs and challenges. This process, she explained, required continuous dialogue, mutual respect, and a shared commitment to the common good.

Back in Kasama, Chilufya and his team organized a community forum to share their insights and foster a deeper understanding of multi-level governance among their fellow villagers. They invited local councilors, traditional leaders, and representatives from nearby villages to participate in the discussion.

The forum was a lively event, filled with passionate debates and thoughtful reflections. Villagers shared their experiences and concerns, while local officials explained how they worked within the broader governance framework to address these issues. The dialogue fostered a sense of unity and collective responsibility, reinforcing the idea that effective governance required everyone's participation.

As the sun set, casting a warm glow over the gathering, Chilufya stood to address the crowd. "We have learned that building better communities is not just about implementing policies; it's about understanding and embracing the connections between all levels of governance. Our strength lies in our unity, in our ability to work together towards a common goal."

With the "Building Better Communities" handbook as their guide, Chilufya and his team felt confident in their ability to navigate the complexities of multi-level governance. They understood that by fostering strong relationships between the national, provincial, and local levels, they could create a governance system that was responsive, inclusive, and effective.

Under the star-lit sky, Chilufya and his team reflected on their journey. They had seen firsthand the power of collaboration and the importance of understanding the roles and responsibilities of different government levels. With renewed determination, they vowed to continue working towards a brighter future, confident in their ability to build a strong, unified community.

Multi-level Governance: Federal, State, and Local Dynamics

"Bridges Across Levels"

The dawn was breaking over Kasama, casting a warm, golden glow on the bustling village. Chilufya and his team gathered under the ancient baobab tree once more, the "Building Better Communities" handbook open before them. Today's discussion would focus on the intricate relationships in multi-level governance, particularly how federal, state, and local dynamics interacted to shape policy and community life.

Chilufya began by explaining that in federal systems, governance was shared between different levels of government, each with its own set of responsibilities and powers. Understanding these dynamics was crucial for effectively implementing policies that addressed the needs of their community.

Determined to gain a comprehensive understanding, Chilufya and his team planned a series of visits. They would journey to Lusaka, the national capital, to learn about federal-level decision-making, then to the provincial capital to understand state-level dynamics, and finally, they would reflect on how these layers interacted with local governance in Kasama.

Their first stop was Lusaka, where they met with Mrs. Ng'andu, a seasoned federal policy advisor. In the grand halls of the Ministry of National Development, Mrs. Ng'andu welcomed them warmly. She explained the federal government's role in creating broad policies that set the direction for the entire country. These policies covered areas like national defense, foreign affairs, and macroeconomic regulation.

Chilufya asked about the challenges of coordinating policies across different levels of government. Mrs. Ng'andu explained that while the federal government provided the framework, it relied on state and local governments to adapt these policies to their specific contexts. This required constant communication and collaboration to ensure that the policies were effectively implemented and met the diverse needs of various regions.

Next, they traveled to the provincial capital, where they met with Mr. Lungu, the head of the Provincial Development Office. Mr. Lungu described how the state government acted as a crucial intermediary, translating federal policies into actionable plans that suited the regional context. He emphasized the importance of understanding local nuances and leveraging state resources to address specific challenges.

Mr. Lungu took them to visit a regional planning meeting, where representatives from different districts gathered to discuss the implementation of a new healthcare policy. Chilufya and his team observed as local officials shared their insights and concerns, providing valuable feedback that would be used to tailor the policy more effectively.

Armed with a deeper understanding of federal and state dynamics, Chilufya and his team returned to Kasama, eager to explore how these levels of governance interacted with their local reality. They organized a community forum, inviting local councilors, traditional leaders, and representatives from neighboring villages to join the discussion.

During the forum, Chilufya explained what they had learned about the federal and state roles. He highlighted how local governance played a critical part in adapting and implementing these policies. Local leaders shared their experiences, discussing the challenges of aligning national and state policies with the unique needs of their community.

One of the local councilors, Mrs. Chanda, spoke passionately about the importance of local engagement in the policy process. She described how the council worked to ensure that national and state initiatives were effectively communicated and implemented on the ground. She also emphasized the need for continuous feedback loops, where local experiences could inform higher levels of governance.

The dialogue at the forum was rich and enlightening. Villagers shared their perspectives, expressing both their hopes and concerns. Through this exchange, it became clear that effective governance required a harmonious interplay between all levels, where each understood and respected the roles and contributions of the others.

As the sun set, Chilufya stood to address the gathering. "We have learned that our strength lies in our ability to bridge the different levels of governance. By understanding and respecting the roles of the federal, state, and local governments, we can work together to build a cohesive and responsive governance system."

With the "Building Better Communities" handbook as their guide, Chilufya and his team felt more equipped than ever to navigate the complexities of multi-level governance. They knew that by fostering strong relationships across all levels of government, they could create policies that were not only well-designed but also effectively implemented, addressing the unique needs of their community.

Under the starlit sky, Chilufya and his team reflected on their journey. They had seen the importance of collaboration and mutual respect between federal, state, and local levels. With renewed determination, they vowed to continue building bridges across these levels, confident in their ability to create a stronger, more unified community.

Public-Private Partnerships in Governance

"Collaborative Paths"

In the vibrant village of Kasama, the sun had just risen, casting a warm glow over the fields and homes. Chilufya and his team gathered under the ancient baobab tree, ready to explore the next critical aspect of governance: public-private partnerships (PPPs). With the "Building Better Communities" handbook open, they prepared to delve into how collaborations between government and private entities could drive sustainable development.

Chilufya began by explaining the concept of public-private partnerships. He highlighted that PPPs combined the strengths of both sectors—government oversight and private sector efficiency—to tackle community challenges effectively. These collaborations could bring in the necessary resources, expertise, and innovation to address issues that were difficult to solve through public efforts alone.

Determined to understand the practical aspects of PPPs, Chilufya and his team decided to visit Lusaka, where several successful PPP projects had been implemented. Their first stop was a newly built healthcare facility, a product of collaboration between the government and a private healthcare provider.

At the healthcare center, they were welcomed by Dr. Tembo, the project manager, who explained how the partnership was formed. The government provided the land and regulatory support, while the private company brought in medical expertise, funding, and state-of-the-art equipment. Together, they had created a facility that offered high-quality medical services to the community.

Dr. Tembo led them on a tour of the center, showcasing the advanced technology and well-trained staff. He emphasized that the success of the project relied on clear communication, shared goals, and mutual respect between the public and private partners. He also mentioned that the private sector's involvement ensured better management and efficiency, crucial for the facility's sustainability.

Inspired by this model, Chilufya and his team returned to Kasama, brimming with ideas for potential PPPs in their village. They organized a meeting with local business leaders, traditional leaders, and council members to discuss how similar partnerships could be formed to address their community's needs.

At the meeting, Chilufya presented the idea of developing a clean water project through a public-private partnership. He proposed collaborating with a local bottling company that had the necessary expertise and resources. The company could provide the technology and infrastructure for water purification, while the government would facilitate the project by granting land and regulatory support.

The business leaders, intrigued by the idea, expressed their willingness to participate. One of them, Mr. Mwape, the owner of the bottling company, saw the potential for both community development and business growth. He agreed to a partnership, promising to bring in the necessary equipment and technical know-how.

Together, they drafted a detailed plan, outlining the roles

and responsibilities of each partner. They agreed to regular meetings to monitor progress and address any challenges collaboratively. This ensured transparency and accountability, fostering a sense of shared ownership over the project.

As the project took off, Chilufya and his team witnessed the transformative power of public-private partnerships. The clean water project progressed smoothly, bringing safe drinking water to every household in Kasama. The villagers, initially skeptical, saw the tangible benefits and became strong supporters of the initiative.

The success of the water project inspired more PPPs in Kasama. A local school partnered with a telecommunications company to provide internet access and digital learning tools, bridging the educational gap. A waste management company collaborated with the local council to implement a sustainable recycling program, improving sanitation and creating jobs.

Under the baobab tree, Chilufya and his team reflected on their journey. They had learned that public-private partnerships could drive significant positive change by leveraging the strengths of both sectors. With the "Building Better Communities" handbook as their guide, they had successfully navigated the complexities of PPPs, transforming their village and setting an example for others.

As the sun set, casting a serene glow over Kasama, Chilufya stood before the gathered villagers. "We have seen that by working together—government, businesses, and community—we can achieve great things. Our partnerships have brought new opportunities and improved our lives. Let us continue to collaborate and build a brighter future for all."

With unity, determination, and a commitment to collaboration, Chilufya and his team were ready to face whatever challenges lay ahead. They knew that by embracing public-private partnerships, they could continue to drive sustainable development and build a stronger, more resilient community.

4

Chapter 4: Economic Policy for Community Development

Macroeconomic Policies: Fiscal and Monetary Tools

"Economic Pillars"

The morning sun cast long shadows over the village of Kasama as Chilufya and his team gathered under the familiar baobab tree. Today, they were about to embark on an exploration of economic policies, specifically focusing on macroeconomic tools that could drive community development. With the "Building Better Communities" handbook in hand, they prepared to dive into the complexities of fiscal and monetary policies.

Chilufya began by explaining the basics of macroeconomic policies, emphasizing that these tools were essential for maintaining economic stability and promoting growth. Fiscal policies involved government spending and taxation, while monetary policies were concerned with controlling the money

40

supply and interest rates. Both sets of policies played a critical role in shaping the economic environment.

To understand these concepts better, Chilufya and his team decided to visit Lusaka, where they would meet with experts at the Ministry of Finance and the Bank of Zambia. They aimed to gain insights into how these policies were crafted and implemented at the national level and how they could be applied to foster community development in Kasama.

Their first stop was the Ministry of Finance, where they met with Mr. Mwila, a senior economic advisor. In his office, filled with charts and economic reports, Mr. Mwila welcomed them warmly and began explaining fiscal policy. He described how the government decided on its budget, allocating funds to various sectors such as education, healthcare, and infrastructure. He also discussed taxation policies and how they influenced economic behavior.

Chilufya asked how these national fiscal policies could impact local communities like Kasama. Mr. Mwila explained that effective fiscal policy could provide the necessary resources for local development projects. For example, increased government spending on rural healthcare and education could directly improve the quality of life in Kasama.

Next, they visited the Bank of Zambia, where they met with Ms. Kunda, an expert in monetary policy. She took them on a tour of the central bank, explaining how monetary policy was used to control inflation, stabilize the currency, and promote economic growth. She highlighted the importance of setting interest rates and regulating the money supply to ensure a stable economic environment.

Ms. Kunda illustrated how these policies impacted local economies. By controlling inflation, the central bank ensured that the value of money remained stable, protecting the purchasing power of the villagers in Kasama. She also discussed how lower interest rates could encourage investment in local businesses, driving economic growth and creating jobs.

Armed with this newfound knowledge, Chilufya and his team returned to Kasama, eager to apply what they had learned. They organized a community meeting to discuss how macroeconomic policies could be leveraged for local development. Villagers, local business owners, and council members gathered under the baobab tree, ready to listen and engage.

Chilufya explained the basics of fiscal and monetary policies in simple terms, emphasizing their importance for community development. He highlighted how government spending on infrastructure could improve roads and access to markets, while educational investments could enhance skills and job opportunities.

One of the local farmers, Mr. Banda, raised a concern about the impact of inflation on his purchasing power. Chilufya shared what he had learned from Ms. Kunda, explaining how the central bank's efforts to control inflation helped protect the value of money, ensuring that farmers like Mr. Banda could afford the goods and services they needed.

Another villager, Mrs. Tembo, asked about how lower interest rates could benefit small businesses. Chilufya explained that with lower interest rates, local entrepreneurs could borrow money at more affordable rates, allowing them to invest in their businesses, expand operations, and create jobs for the community.

Inspired by the discussion, the villagers decided to take proactive steps. They formed a local economic development committee to liaise with government officials and advocate for increased investment in their community. They also worked on developing proposals for infrastructure projects and educational programs that could be funded through fiscal policy initiatives.

Under the baobab tree, Chilufya and his team reflected on their journey. They had learned that macroeconomic policies were powerful tools for shaping the economic landscape and driving community development. With the "Building Better Communities" handbook as their guide, they were confident in their ability to harness these tools to build a stronger, more resilient Kasama.

As the sun set, casting a warm glow over the village, Chilufya stood before the gathered community. "We have seen that by understanding and leveraging fiscal and monetary policies, we can drive sustainable development and improve our quality of life. Let us continue to work together, using these economic tools to build a brighter future for all."

With unity, determination, and a commitment to economic understanding, Chilufya and his team were ready to face whatever challenges lay ahead. They knew that by embracing macroeconomic policies, they could foster sustainable growth and create a thriving community.

Economic Growth Strategies

"Paths to Prosperity"

In the heart of Kasama, the morning air buzzed with anticipation as Chilufya and his team gathered once again under the ancient baobab tree. They were ready to explore the next crucial element of economic policy for community development: economic growth strategies. With the "Building Better Communities" handbook in hand, they aimed to uncover the pathways to sustainable prosperity for their village.

Chilufya began by explaining that economic growth strategies were plans and policies designed to promote sustained increases in economic activity and improve living standards. These strategies could involve various approaches, such as investing in infrastructure, promoting entrepreneurship, enhancing education and skills, and leveraging natural resources responsibly.

To gain a deeper understanding, Chilufya and his team decided to visit several successful projects and initiatives in Zambia that had effectively implemented growth strategies. Their journey took them to Kitwe, the economic hub of the Copperbelt Province, where they hoped to learn from ongoing industrial and agricultural projects.

Their first stop was a large-scale agricultural cooperative known for its innovative farming techniques and strong community involvement. They were greeted by Ms. Mwansa, the cooperative's manager, who enthusiastically shared their story. She explained how the cooperative had transformed local agriculture by introducing modern farming practices, investing in irrigation systems, and providing training programs for farmers.

Ms. Mwansa took them on a tour of the fields, where they saw crops thriving under efficient irrigation and farmers using new tools and techniques. She emphasized that the cooperative's success was built on continuous learning, community participation, and strategic investments. By focusing on high-value crops and improving productivity, they had significantly increased their output and incomes.

Chilufya asked about the challenges they had faced and how they had overcome them. Ms. Mwansa mentioned initial resistance to change and the need for significant upfront investment. However, through persistent efforts, education, and demonstrating tangible benefits, they had gradually won over the community and attracted necessary funding.

Next, the team visited an industrial park in Kitwe that had become a model for economic diversification. There, they met Mr. Phiri, the director of the industrial park, who explained how they had attracted various industries, from manufacturing to technology startups, creating a robust economic ecosystem.

Mr. Phiri highlighted the importance of infrastructure development, such as reliable power supply, good transportation networks, and effective communication systems, in attracting businesses. He also stressed the role of government incentives, such as tax breaks and grants, in encouraging investment and innovation.

Armed with these insights, Chilufya and his team returned to Kasama, inspired and determined to implement effective economic growth strategies. They organized a village meeting to share their experiences and discuss how similar strategies could be applied to their community.

Under the baobab tree, Chilufya presented the key lessons they had learned. He emphasized the importance of investing in infrastructure, promoting entrepreneurship, enhancing education and skills, and leveraging their natural resources responsibly. He suggested forming a local economic development committee to spearhead these initiatives.

One of the local entrepreneurs, Mrs. Chisanga, proposed starting a small business incubator to support local startups and foster innovation. She shared her vision of creating a space where aspiring entrepreneurs could access training, mentorship, and resources to turn their ideas into viable businesses.

The villagers embraced the idea enthusiastically. They discussed potential projects, such as improving irrigation systems for agriculture, setting up vocational training centers, and promoting eco-tourism to attract visitors to their beautiful region. They also talked about the importance of sustainable practices to protect their natural environment.

The local councilors pledged their support, promising to seek funding and collaborate with regional and national authorities to implement these growth strategies. They agreed to work closely with the newly formed economic development committee, ensuring that all initiatives were community-driven and aligned with their needs and aspirations.

As the sun set, casting a warm glow over the village, Chilufya stood before the gathered community. "We have learned that by adopting effective economic growth strategies, we can create sustainable prosperity for our village. Let us work together, invest in our future, and build a thriving community for generations to come."

With unity, determination, and a commitment to strategic planning, Chilufya and his team felt confident in their ability to drive economic growth and improve living standards in Kasama. They knew that by leveraging their strengths, embracing innovation, and working together, they could pave the way to a brighter, more prosperous future.

Employment and Labor Policies

"Building a Workforce, Building a Future"

The first light of dawn touched the horizon as Chilufya and his team assembled once more under the ancient baobab tree in Kasama. The "Building Better Communities" handbook lay open, ready to guide them through their next critical topic: employment and labor policies. Understanding these policies was vital for fostering a robust and inclusive workforce in their village.

Chilufya began by explaining the significance of employment and labor policies. These policies were designed to create job opportunities, ensure fair wages, and protect workers' rights. They were essential for building a productive, motivated, and sustainable workforce that could drive community development.

To gain practical insights, Chilufya and his team decided to visit Lusaka and Ndola, two cities known for their progressive employment initiatives. They aimed to learn from successful programs and bring back ideas to implement in Kasama.

Their first stop was Lusaka, where they met with Ms. Mwewa, the head of a government-backed job training program. The program, called "Skills for Growth," provided vocational training to young people and adults, equipping them with skills in various trades such as carpentry, plumbing, and computer technology.

Ms. Mwewa welcomed them warmly and explained the program's impact. "We realized that many young people lacked the skills needed to find stable employment," she said. "By offering targeted training programs, we are not only helping individuals but also boosting the local economy."

She took them on a tour of the training center, where they saw students engrossed in hands-on learning. Chilufya was particularly impressed by the partnerships the program had formed with local businesses, ensuring that the training was aligned with market needs and that graduates could easily find jobs.

Chilufya asked about the challenges they faced. Ms. Mwewa admitted that securing funding and maintaining up-to-date equipment were ongoing issues, but the community's support and the program's tangible results had helped overcome many obstacles.

Next, the team traveled to Ndola, where they visited a large manufacturing plant known for its progressive labor policies. There, they met Mr. Banda, the plant manager, who proudly shared how they had created a supportive work environment that prioritized employee well-being.

Mr. Banda explained their approach to fair wages, safe working conditions, and employee benefits. "We believe that when we take care of our employees, they are more productive and loyal," he said. He also highlighted their worker training programs, which offered continuous education and opportunities for advancement.

Chilufya was struck by the sense of pride and satisfaction among the workers they spoke with. He saw firsthand how good labor policies could create a motivated and efficient workforce, benefiting both the employees and the company.

With these valuable lessons in mind, Chilufya and his team returned to Kasama, ready to develop and implement effective employment and labor policies. They organized a community meeting under the baobab tree, inviting local business owners, council members, and villagers to discuss the way forward.

Chilufya shared the insights they had gathered. He emphasized the importance of vocational training to equip villagers with marketable skills and the need for fair wages and safe working conditions to create a motivated workforce. He proposed setting up a local training center similar to the one in Lusaka and encouraging local businesses to adopt better labor practices.

One of the local business owners, Mr. Mutale, voiced his support. "I have always believed that investing in my employees is good for business. I am willing to collaborate on creating a training program that benefits everyone."

The villagers were enthusiastic about the idea. They discussed potential training programs, such as tailoring, welding, and computer skills, and explored ways to fund the initiative. They also agreed on the importance of enforcing fair labor practices and ensuring that all workers were treated with dignity and respect.

The local councilors pledged their support, promising to secure funding and collaborate with regional and national authorities to implement these employment and labor policies. They agreed to work closely with the community, ensuring that all initiatives were inclusive and aligned with their needs and aspirations.

As the sun set, casting a warm glow over the village, Chilufya stood before the gathered community. "We have learned that by implementing effective employment and labor policies, we can create a strong, motivated workforce that drives our community's growth. Let us work together, invest in our people, and build a brighter future for all."

With unity, determination, and a commitment to fair

employment practices, Chilufya and his team felt confident in their ability to create a thriving workforce in Kasama. They knew that by leveraging their strengths, embracing innovation, and working together, they could pave the way to a brighter, more prosperous future.

Income Inequality and Poverty Alleviation

"Bridging the Gap"

The golden morning light filtered through the leaves of the ancient baobab tree in Kasama, where Chilufya and his team once again gathered. The "Building Better Communities" handbook lay open before them, ready to guide their exploration of a critical issue: income inequality and poverty alleviation. They understood that addressing these challenges was key to fostering a just and thriving community.

Chilufya began by explaining the significance of addressing income inequality and poverty. He highlighted that reducing the gap between the rich and the poor and ensuring that everyone had access to basic needs were essential for sustainable development and social cohesion.

Determined to find practical solutions, Chilufya and his team decided to visit several successful poverty alleviation programs across Zambia. Their first destination was the rural district of Chongwe, where a community-driven initiative had made significant strides in reducing poverty and inequality.

In Chongwe, they were welcomed by Mrs. Kabwe, the coordinator of a local microfinance program. She explained how the program provided small loans to women and marginalized groups, enabling them to start their own businesses. "By giving people the tools to become self-sufficient, we can break the cycle of poverty," she said.

Mrs. Kabwe took them to meet some of the beneficiaries. Chilufya and his team were inspired by the stories of women who had used the loans to start small enterprises, such as tailoring shops, vegetable gardens, and poultry farms. These businesses not only provided a steady income but also created jobs and strengthened the local economy.

One beneficiary, Mrs. Zulu, shared her story. "Before the loan, I struggled to feed my children. Now, my vegetable business is thriving, and I can afford to send them to school. This program has changed our lives."

Next, the team traveled to Livingstone, where they visited a successful social enterprise focused on education and skills development. There, they met Mr. Mwamba, the founder of the organization, who explained their approach to poverty alleviation. "Education is the key to breaking the cycle of poverty. We provide free schooling and vocational training to the poorest families, giving them the tools to build a better future."

Mr. Mwamba took them on a tour of the facility, where they saw children and young adults engaged in various learning activities. Chilufya was impressed by the comprehensive support system, which included not only education but also healthcare, nutrition, and counseling services.

Armed with these insights, Chilufya and his team returned to Kasama, determined to implement effective strategies to reduce income inequality and alleviate poverty. They organized a community meeting under the baobab tree, inviting local leaders, business owners, and villagers to discuss their findings and brainstorm solutions.

Chilufya shared the success stories from Chongwe and Livingstone, emphasizing the importance of empowering marginalized groups and investing in education and skills development. He proposed establishing a microfinance program in Kasama, similar to the one in Chongwe, and creating a community center that offered education and vocational training.

One of the local leaders, Chief Nkandu, voiced his support. "We have seen the impact of poverty on our community. By working together and implementing these strategies, we can create opportunities for everyone and ensure that no one is left behind."

The villagers were enthusiastic about the ideas. They discussed potential projects, such as forming savings and loan groups, offering business training, and setting up scholarships for children from low-income families. They also agreed on the importance of creating a support network to help people overcome challenges and achieve their goals.

The local councilors pledged their support, promising to secure funding and collaborate with regional and national authorities to implement these initiatives. They agreed to work closely with the community, ensuring that all efforts were inclusive and focused on the most vulnerable members.

As the sun set, casting a warm glow over the village, Chilufya stood before the gathered community. "We have learned that by addressing income inequality and poverty, we can build a more just and prosperous society. Let us work together, empower each other, and create a future where everyone has the opportunity to thrive."

With unity, determination, and a commitment to social justice, Chilufya and his team felt confident in their ability to reduce income inequality and alleviate poverty in Kasama. They knew that by leveraging their strengths, embracing innovation, and working together, they could bridge the gap and create a brighter, more equitable future for all.

Innovation and Entrepreneurship Policies

"Seeds of Innovation"

As the sun began its ascent over Kasama, casting a warm glow over the bustling village, Chilufya and his team gathered once more under the shade of the ancient baobab tree. With the "Building Better Communities" handbook as their guide, they prepared to delve into the transformative power of innovation and entrepreneurship policies in driving economic growth and prosperity.

Chilufya began by explaining the importance of fostering a culture of innovation and entrepreneurship in Kasama. He highlighted that these policies could spark creativity, drive job creation, and catalyze economic development, ultimately leading to a more vibrant and resilient community.

Eager to explore practical examples, Chilufya and his team set out on a journey to visit innovative initiatives and entrepreneurial ventures across Zambia. Their first destination was the capital city of Lusaka, where they hoped to learn from successful startups and supportive innovation ecosystems.

In Lusaka, they were welcomed by Mr. Mulenga, the founder of a technology incubator that supported aspiring entrepreneurs in developing their ideas into viable businesses. Mr. Mulenga shared his vision of creating a thriving startup ecosystem that would drive Zambia's economic transformation.

He took them on a tour of the incubator, where they met with several young entrepreneurs working on innovative solutions to local challenges. From mobile payment platforms to solar-powered irrigation systems, Chilufya and his team were inspired by the creativity and determination of the startup founders.

One entrepreneur, Ms. Tembo, explained how the support and mentorship provided by the incubator had helped her turn her idea for a healthcare app into a reality. "With access to funding, guidance, and networking opportunities, I was able to overcome obstacles and bring my vision to life," she said.

Next, the team traveled to Ndola, where they visited a successful manufacturing company that had embraced innovation to stay competitive in the global market. There, they met with Mr. Bwalya, the CEO, who shared their approach to fostering creativity and embracing new technologies.

Mr. Bwalya explained how they had invested in research and development, encouraged experimentation, and created a culture that rewarded innovation. "Innovation is the lifeblood of our company," he said. "By constantly pushing the boundaries of what is possible, we stay ahead of the curve and create value for our customers."

Impressed by what they had seen, Chilufya and his team returned to Kasama, determined to nurture a culture of innovation and entrepreneurship in their own community. They organized a gathering under the baobab tree, inviting local leaders, business owners, and aspiring entrepreneurs to share ideas and collaborate on solutions.

Chilufya shared the success stories they had encountered in Lusaka and Ndola, emphasizing the importance of providing support and resources to enable local innovators to thrive. He proposed establishing a local innovation hub where entrepreneurs could access funding, mentorship, and networking opportunities.

One aspiring entrepreneur, Mr. Musonda, shared his idea for a sustainable agriculture startup that would use innovative techniques to improve crop yields and reduce environmental impact. "With the right support, I believe we can create solutions that benefit both our community and the planet," he said.

The villagers were enthusiastic about the idea. They discussed potential projects, such as a community-led innovation fund, training programs for aspiring entrepreneurs, and partnerships with local universities and businesses.

The local councilors pledged their support, promising to allocate resources and create a supportive regulatory environment for innovation and entrepreneurship to flourish. They agreed to work closely with the community, ensuring that all initiatives were inclusive and aligned with their needs and aspirations.

As the sun set, casting a warm glow over the village, Chilufya stood before the gathered community. "We have learned that by fostering a culture of innovation and entrepreneurship, we can unleash the potential of our community and create new opportunities for growth and prosperity. Let us work together, nurture our creativity, and build a brighter future for all."

With unity, determination, and a commitment to innovation, Chilufya and his team felt confident in their ability to drive economic development and create a more vibrant and resilient Kasama. They knew that by embracing creativity, embracing change, and working together, they could plant the seeds of innovation that would blossom into a brighter tomorrow.

Sustainable Development and Environmental Economics

"Harmony with Nature"

As the sun rose over Kasama, painting the sky with hues of orange and pink, Chilufya and his team gathered beneath the sprawling branches of the ancient baobab tree. Today, they would explore the vital connection between sustainable development and environmental economics—a cornerstone of building a resilient and thriving community.

Chilufya began by underlining the intrinsic link between economic prosperity and environmental stewardship. He explained that sustainable development aimed to meet the needs of the present without compromising the ability of future generations to meet their own needs. Environmental economics, therefore, sought to integrate environmental considerations into economic decision-making to ensure long-term ecological balance and human well-being.

To grasp these concepts in action, Chilufya and his team embarked on a journey to visit sustainable development initiatives and environmental conservation projects across Zambia. Their first destination was the Kafue National Park, a pristine wilderness teeming with diverse flora and fauna.

In the heart of the park, they were greeted by Ms. Ngoma, a

passionate conservationist dedicated to preserving Zambia's natural heritage. Ms. Ngoma led them on a guided tour, showcasing the park's rich biodiversity and discussing the challenges and opportunities of balancing conservation with economic development.

As they walked through the lush forest and watched herds of elephants and zebras roam freely, Chilufya and his team gained a profound appreciation for the delicate harmony between humans and nature. Ms. Ngoma emphasized the importance of sustainable tourism as a source of revenue for conservation efforts while promoting environmental education and awareness among visitors.

Next, the team traveled to the Copperbelt Province, where they visited a community-led reforestation project. There, they met Mr. Chanda, a local farmer who had mobilized his community to plant trees and restore degraded land.

Mr. Chanda explained how deforestation and soil erosion had threatened their livelihoods, prompting them to take action. With support from government agencies and NGOs, they had established nurseries, implemented agroforestry practices, and engaged in sustainable land management techniques.

Witnessing the transformation of barren landscapes into thriving forests filled Chilufya and his team with hope and inspiration. They realized that sustainable development was not only about economic growth but also about preserving natural resources for future generations.

Armed with these insights, Chilufya and his team returned to Kasama, determined to integrate principles of sustainable development and environmental economics into their community's economic policies. They convened a meeting under the baobab tree, inviting local leaders, farmers, and environmental activists to join the conversation.

Chilufya shared the lessons they had learned from Kafue National Park and the reforestation project, stressing the importance of protecting Kasama's natural resources while promoting economic growth. He proposed initiatives such as sustainable agriculture practices, eco-friendly tourism, and renewable energy projects that would create jobs and preserve the environment.

One of the local farmers, Mrs. Mwape, shared her experience implementing agroforestry techniques on her land. "By planting trees alongside our crops, we have improved soil fertility, increased crop yields, and provided habitat for wildlife," she said. "Sustainable farming benefits both our community and the environment."

The villagers expressed their support for the proposed initiatives, recognizing the importance of living in harmony with nature. They discussed ways to conserve water resources, protect biodiversity, and reduce pollution while promoting economic development.

The local councilors pledged their support, promising to allocate resources and enact policies that promoted sustainable development and environmental conservation. They agreed to work closely with the community, ensuring that all initiatives were inclusive and aligned with their values and aspirations.

As the sun set, casting a golden glow over the village, Chilufya stood before the gathered community. "We have learned that by embracing sustainable development and environmental economics, we can create a future where our community thrives in harmony with nature," he said. "Let us work together, stewarding our resources wisely, and build a brighter tomorrow for generations to come."

With unity, determination, and a commitment to sustainability, Chilufya and his team felt empowered to lead Kasama towards a future where economic prosperity and environmental preservation went hand in hand. They knew that by embracing the principles of sustainable development, they could create a resilient and thriving community that flourished for years to come.

5

Chapter 5: Social Policy and Equity

Healthcare Policy and Access to Services

"Healing Hands"

U nder the canopy of the ancient baobab tree, the air in Kasama was charged with anticipation as Chilufya and his team convened once more. Today, their focus shifted to the vital realm of social policy and equity, with a specific emphasis on healthcare policy and access to services. With the "Building Better Communities" handbook as their compass, they embarked on a journey to explore how equitable healthcare could transform lives and strengthen their community.

Chilufya opened the discussion by emphasizing that access to quality healthcare was a fundamental human right and a cornerstone of a just and equitable society. He stressed the importance of healthcare policy in ensuring that all members of the community could receive the care they needed, regardless of their socio-economic status.

To gain practical insights, Chilufya and his team set out to visit healthcare facilities and initiatives that were making a difference in communities across Zambia. Their first stop was the bustling city of Kitwe, where they hoped to learn from innovative healthcare programs that prioritized accessibility and inclusivity.

In Kitwe, they were welcomed by Dr. Mulenga, the director of a community health center that provided comprehensive healthcare services to residents, including primary care, maternal and child health, and infectious disease management.

Dr. Mulenga led them on a tour of the facility, where they witnessed dedicated healthcare workers providing compassionate care to patients from all walks of life. From routine check-ups to life-saving treatments, the center was a beacon of hope for those in need.

As they spoke with patients and caregivers, Chilufya and his team learned about the challenges of delivering healthcare in resource-constrained settings and the innovative solutions that had been implemented to overcome them.

Next, the team traveled to the rural district of Choma, where they visited a mobile clinic that brought healthcare services to remote villages and underserved communities. There, they met Nurse Banda, who explained how the mobile clinic had revolutionized healthcare delivery in the area.

Nurse Banda described how the clinic provided vaccinations, screenings, and basic treatments to villagers who would otherwise have limited access to medical care. She emphasized the importance of preventive healthcare and community engagement in improving health outcomes.

Moved by what they had witnessed, Chilufya and his team

returned to Kasama, determined to apply the lessons learned to their own community. They organized a meeting under the baobab tree, inviting local leaders, healthcare workers, and community members to join the conversation.

Chilufya shared the success stories from Kitwe and Choma, highlighting the importance of accessible and inclusive healthcare services. He proposed initiatives such as mobile clinics, community health workers, and health education programs that would bring healthcare closer to the people.

One of the local nurses, Sister Mulenga, shared her experience working in Kasama's health center and the challenges they faced in providing care to remote villages. "By bringing healthcare services directly to the communities, we can reach more people and address their needs in a timely manner," she said.

The villagers expressed their support for the proposed initiatives, recognizing the importance of healthcare in building a healthy and resilient community. They discussed ways to improve access to healthcare, promote preventive measures, and empower individuals to take control of their health.

The local councilors pledged their support, promising to allocate resources and collaborate with healthcare professionals to implement these initiatives. They agreed to work closely with the community, ensuring that all efforts were inclusive and aligned with their needs and priorities.

As the sun set, casting a warm glow over the village, Chilufya stood before the gathered community. "We have learned that by prioritizing healthcare policy and improving access to services, we can build a healthier and more equitable community," he said. "Let us work together, ensuring that no one is left behind, and that everyone has the opportunity to live a full and healthy life."

With unity, determination, and a commitment to equity, Chilufya and his team felt empowered to lead Kasama towards a future where healthcare was accessible to all. They knew that by embracing the principles of social policy and equity, they could create a community where every individual could thrive and flourish.

Education Policies for Equal Opportunity

"Enlightening Paths"

Beneath the sprawling branches of the ancient baobab tree, the air in Kasama was filled with a sense of anticipation as Chilufya and his team reconvened once more. Today, their focus shifted to the transformative realm of education policies for equal opportunity. With the "Building Better Communities" handbook as their guide, they embarked on a journey to explore how access to quality education could break down barriers and pave the way for a brighter future for all.

Chilufya opened the discussion by highlighting that education was the cornerstone of empowerment and social mobility. He stressed the importance of education policies that ensured equal access to quality learning opportunities, regardless of background or circumstance.

To gain practical insights, Chilufya and his team set out to visit schools and educational initiatives that were making a difference in communities across Zambia. Their first destination was the capital city of Lusaka, where they hoped to learn from innovative education programs that prioritized inclusivity and excellence.

In Lusaka, they were welcomed by Ms. Nkosi, the head-teacher of a public school that had earned acclaim for its student-centered approach to learning. Ms. Nkosi led them on a tour of the school, where they witnessed engaged students and passionate teachers working together to create a nurturing learning environment.

As they observed classrooms bustling with activity and heard stories of academic achievement and personal growth, Chilufya and his team gained a profound appreciation for the transformative power of education. Ms. Nkosi emphasized the importance of individualized support and personalized learning plans in meeting the diverse needs of students.

Next, the team traveled to the rural district of Monze, where they visited a community-led initiative focused on girls' education. There, they met Ms. Chanda, a dedicated educator who had established a scholarship program to support girls from disadvantaged backgrounds.

Ms. Chanda shared her own journey of overcoming obstacles to pursue her education and how she was determined to create opportunities for other girls to do the same. She emphasized the importance of gender equality in education and the role of mentorship and support networks in empowering young women.

Moved by what they had witnessed, Chilufya and his team returned to Kasama, determined to apply the lessons learned to their own community. They organized a meeting under the baobab tree, inviting local leaders, educators, and community members to join the conversation.

Chilufya shared the success stories from Lusaka and Monze, highlighting the importance of inclusive education policies that catered to the diverse needs of learners. He proposed initiatives such as scholarships, mentorship programs, and community engagement activities that would break down barriers to education and ensure equal opportunities for all.

One of the local teachers, Mr. Bwalya, shared his experience working in Kasama's schools and the challenges they faced in providing quality education to every child. "By investing in teacher training, infrastructure development, and curriculum reform, we can create a learning environment where every child can thrive," he said.

The villagers expressed their support for the proposed initiatives, recognizing the importance of education in unlocking potential and building a brighter future. They discussed ways to improve school infrastructure, expand access to early childhood education, and promote lifelong learning opportunities for all members of the community.

The local councilors pledged their support, promising to allocate resources and collaborate with educators and community leaders to implement these initiatives. They agreed to work closely with the community, ensuring that all efforts were inclusive and aligned with their needs and aspirations.

As the sun set, casting a warm glow over the village, Chilufya stood before the gathered community. "We have learned that by prioritizing education policies for equal opportunity, we can unlock the potential of every child and build a more just and prosperous society," he said. "Let us work together, ensuring that every child has the chance to reach their full potential and contribute to our community's success."

With unity, determination, and a commitment to excellence, Chilufya and his team felt empowered to lead Kasama towards a future where education was a pathway to opportunity for all. They knew that by embracing the principles of social policy and equity, they could create a community where every individual could thrive and flourish.

Housing and Urban Development Strategies

"Building Dreams, Building Communities"

Under the wide canopy of the ancient baobab tree, the atmosphere in Kasama buzzed with excitement as Chilufya and his team gathered once more. Today, their focus shifted to the critical domain of housing and urban development strategies—a cornerstone of social policy and equity. With the "Building Better Communities" handbook guiding their path, they embarked on a journey to explore how access to safe and affordable housing could transform lives and foster inclusive communities.

Chilufya began by highlighting the fundamental importance of housing in providing stability, security, and dignity to individuals and families. He stressed the need for housing policies and urban development strategies that prioritized affordability, accessibility, and sustainability to ensure that everyone had a place to call home.

To gain practical insights, Chilufya and his team set out to visit housing projects and urban development initiatives across Zambia. Their first destination was the bustling city of Ndola, where they hoped to learn from innovative approaches to addressing the housing crisis and promoting inclusive urbanization.

In Ndola, they were welcomed by Mr. Chanda, the director

of a community-driven housing cooperative that was pioneering a new model of affordable housing. Mr. Chanda led them on a tour of the cooperative's development, where they saw rows of brightly painted houses surrounded by vibrant community spaces.

As they walked through the neighborhood, Chilufya and his team marveled at the sense of pride and belonging among the residents. Mr. Chanda explained how the cooperative had mobilized community members to pool their resources and work together to build homes that met their needs and aspirations.

Next, the team traveled to the rural district of Choma, where they visited a government-led housing project aimed at providing housing for low-income families. There, they met Mrs. Mwinga, a beneficiary of the project, who shared her journey of moving from a makeshift shelter to a safe and dignified home.

Mrs. Mwinga emphasized the transformative impact of having a stable and secure place to live on her family's well-being and future prospects. She expressed gratitude for the support of the government and community in making her dream of homeownership a reality.

Moved by what they had witnessed, Chilufya and his team returned to Kasama, determined to apply the lessons learned to their own community. They organized a meeting under the baobab tree, inviting local leaders, housing advocates, and community members to join the conversation.

Chilufya shared the success stories from Ndola and Choma, highlighting the importance of collaborative and inclusive approaches to housing and urban development. He proposed initiatives such as community-led housing cooperatives, mixed-income developments, and infrastructure investments that would create vibrant and sustainable neighborhoods.

One of the local residents, Mr. Mutale, shared his experience of living in overcrowded and unsafe conditions and the impact it had on his family's health and well-being. "By investing in housing and urban development, we can create communities where everyone has access to safe and affordable housing," he said.

The villagers expressed their support for the proposed initiatives, recognizing the importance of housing in building strong and resilient communities. They discussed ways to improve housing conditions, enhance access to basic services, and promote sustainable urbanization.

The local councilors pledged their support, promising to allocate resources and collaborate with housing experts and community leaders to implement these initiatives. They agreed to work closely with the community, ensuring that all efforts were inclusive and aligned with their needs and aspirations.

As the sun set, casting a warm glow over the village, Chilufya stood before the gathered community. "We have learned that by prioritizing housing and urban development strategies, we can create communities where everyone has a place to call home," he said. "Let us work together, building dreams and building communities, where every individual can thrive and flourish."

With unity, determination, and a commitment to inclusivity, Chilufya and his team felt empowered to lead Kasama towards a future where housing was a foundation for opportunity and prosperity. They knew that by embracing the principles of social policy and equity, they could create a community where everyone had the chance to build a better life for themselves and their families.

Social Welfare Programs and Safety Nets

"Circles of Support"

Underneath the ancient baobab tree, Kasama's villagers gathered, their faces etched with anticipation. Today, Chilufya and his team delved deeper into the realm of social policy and equity, focusing on the pivotal role of social welfare programs and safety nets. With the "Building Better Communities" handbook as their beacon, they embarked on a journey to explore how these initiatives could uplift the most vulnerable and foster a more compassionate society.

Chilufya began by underscoring the importance of social welfare programs as a lifeline for those facing adversity, ensuring that no one was left behind in their journey toward a better life. He emphasized the need for safety nets that provided support, dignity, and hope to individuals and families experiencing hardship.

To gain practical insights, Chilufya and his team set out to visit social welfare programs and safety net initiatives across Zambia. Their first stop was the bustling town of Kabwe, where they hoped to learn from innovative approaches to addressing poverty and inequality.

In Kabwe, they were welcomed by Ms. Mulenga, the coordinator of a community-based program that provided food assistance and social services to vulnerable households. Ms. Mulenga led them through the bustling center, where volunteers distributed nutritious meals, offered counseling services, and connected families with resources and support networks.

As they interacted with program beneficiaries and listened to their stories of resilience and hope, Chilufya and his team were deeply moved by the impact of the program on people's lives. Ms. Mulenga emphasized the importance of holistic support in addressing the root causes of poverty and empowering individuals to build a better future.

Next, the team traveled to the rural village of Luangwa, where they visited a government-run safety net program that provided cash transfers to vulnerable households. There, they met Mr. Phiri, a beneficiary of the program, who shared how the monthly stipend had enabled his family to meet their basic needs and invest in their children's education.

Mr. Phiri expressed gratitude for the support of the government and community in providing a safety net during difficult times. He spoke of the sense of security and dignity that came from knowing that his family had access to essential resources and services.

Inspired by what they had witnessed, Chilufya and his team returned to Kasama, determined to apply the lessons learned to their own community. They organized a meeting under the baobab tree, inviting local leaders, social workers, and community members to join the conversation.

Chilufya shared the success stories from Kabwe and Luangwa, highlighting the importance of social welfare programs and safety nets in providing a cushion against adversity. He proposed initiatives such as food assistance programs, cash transfer schemes, and job training opportunities that would support those in need and promote social inclusion.

One of the local social workers, Mrs. Banda, shared her

experience working with vulnerable families in Kasama and the challenges they faced in accessing essential services. "By expanding social welfare programs and safety nets, we can create a more resilient and compassionate community," she said.

The villagers expressed their support for the proposed initiatives, recognizing the importance of solidarity and support in times of need. They discussed ways to strengthen existing programs, expand outreach efforts, and build a network of community support to uplift those facing hardship.

The local councilors pledged their support, promising to allocate resources and collaborate with social service providers and community organizations to implement these initiatives. They agreed to work closely with the community, ensuring that all efforts were inclusive and responsive to their needs and aspirations.

As the sun set, casting a warm glow over the village, Chilufya stood before the gathered community. "We have learned that by prioritizing social welfare programs and safety nets, we can create a community where everyone has the support and resources they need to thrive," he said. "Let us work together, building circles of support and compassion, where no one is left behind."

With unity, determination, and a commitment to solidarity, Chilufya and his team felt empowered to lead Kasama towards a future where social justice and equity prevailed. They knew that by embracing the principles of social policy and equity, they could create a community where everyone had the opportunity to live with dignity and purpose.

Diversity, Inclusion, and Social Justice Policies

"Bridges of Understanding"

As the sun dipped below the horizon, casting a warm glow over Kasama, Chilufya and his team gathered once more beneath the ancient baobab tree. Today, their focus shifted to the transformative realm of diversity, inclusion, and social justice policies—a cornerstone of building equitable and harmonious communities. With the "Building Better Communities" handbook illuminating their path, they embarked on a journey to explore how embracing diversity and fostering inclusion could create a more just and compassionate society for all.

Chilufya began by emphasizing the intrinsic value of diversity and the importance of creating inclusive communities where everyone felt valued and respected. He stressed the need for policies that promoted social justice, equity, and opportunity for all members of society, regardless of their background or identity.

To gain practical insights, Chilufya and his team set out to explore initiatives and programs that championed diversity, inclusion, and social justice across Zambia. Their first destination was the vibrant city of Livingstone, where they hoped to learn from innovative approaches to promoting diversity and inclusion in a multicultural society.

In Livingstone, they were welcomed by Mr. Sibanda, the coordinator of a community center that celebrated Zambia's rich cultural heritage and promoted intercultural dialogue and understanding. Mr. Sibanda led them on a tour of the center, where they saw exhibits showcasing traditional arts, music, and cuisine from various ethnic groups.

As they immersed themselves in the colorful tapestry of Zambian culture, Chilufya and his team gained a deeper appreciation for the beauty of diversity and the power of dialogue in fostering unity and harmony. Mr. Sibanda emphasized the importance of building bridges of understanding across cultural divides and creating spaces where people from different backgrounds could come together as equals.

Next, the team traveled to the bustling town of Chipata, where they visited a youth-led initiative focused on promoting social justice and equality. There, they met Ms. Phiri, a passionate activist who spoke about the importance of grassroots movements in advocating for change and challenging systemic inequalities.

Ms. Phiri shared her experiences organizing protests, raising awareness about social issues, and mobilizing young people to demand justice and accountability from their leaders. She emphasized the need for policies that addressed the root causes of inequality and discrimination and promoted equal rights and opportunities for all.

Inspired by what they had witnessed, Chilufya and his team returned to Kasama, determined to apply the lessons learned to their own community. They organized a meeting under the baobab tree, inviting local leaders, activists, and community members to join the conversation.

Chilufya shared the success stories from Livingstone and Chipata, highlighting the importance of diversity, inclusion, and social justice in building a more just and compassionate society. He proposed initiatives such as cultural exchange programs, anti-discrimination policies, and youth empowerment initiatives that would promote understanding, respect, and equality among all members of the community.

One of the local activists, Mr. Ngoma, shared his experience advocating for the rights of marginalized groups in Kasama and the need for policies that addressed systemic barriers to inclusion. "By embracing diversity and promoting social justice, we can create a community where everyone feels valued and respected," he said.

The villagers expressed their support for the proposed initiatives, recognizing the importance of unity and solidarity in creating a more equitable and harmonious society. They discussed ways to celebrate diversity, foster intercultural understanding, and dismantle discrimination and prejudice in all its forms.

The local councilors pledged their support, promising to enact policies and allocate resources to promote diversity, inclusion, and social justice in Kasama. They agreed to work closely with the community, ensuring that all efforts were inclusive and responsive to their needs and aspirations.

As the stars twinkled overhead, bathing the village in a soft glow, Chilufya stood before the gathered community. "We have learned that by embracing diversity, fostering inclusion, and promoting social justice, we can create a community where everyone has the opportunity to thrive and flourish," he said. "Let us work together, building bridges of understanding and solidarity, and creating a future where everyone is treated with dignity and respect."

With unity, determination, and a commitment to justice, Chilufya and his team felt empowered to lead Kasama towards a future where diversity was celebrated, inclusion was the norm, and social justice prevailed. They knew that by embracing the principles of social policy and equity, they could create a community where everyone had the chance to live a life of dignity, purpose, and fulfillment.

Promoting Gender Equality

"Empowering Voices"

As the village of Kasama basked in the gentle glow of twilight, Chilufya and his team gathered once more beneath the ancient baobab tree. Today, their focus shifted to the transformative realm of promoting gender equality—a cornerstone of building inclusive and equitable communities. With the "Building Better Communities" handbook as their guiding light, they embarked on a journey to explore how empowering women and promoting gender equality could unlock the full potential of their society.

Chilufya began by highlighting the fundamental importance of gender equality in achieving social justice and fostering sustainable development. He emphasized the need for policies and initiatives that empowered women, challenged gender norms, and created opportunities for all members of society to thrive.

To gain practical insights, Chilufya and his team set out to explore initiatives and programs that promoted gender equality across Zambia. Their first destination was the bustling city of Lusaka, where they hoped to learn from innovative approaches to empowering women and girls in urban settings.

In Lusaka, they were welcomed by Mrs. Banda, the founder of a women's empowerment organization that provided training, mentorship, and support to aspiring female entrepreneurs. Mrs. Banda led them on a tour of the organization's training center, where they met women from diverse backgrounds who were pursuing their dreams of economic independence.

As they listened to the women's stories of resilience and determination, Chilufya and his team were inspired by the transformative impact of empowering women to take control of their lives and livelihoods. Mrs. Banda emphasized the importance of providing women with access to education, skills training, and financial resources to unlock their potential and overcome barriers to success.

Next, the team traveled to the rural village of Lundazi, where they visited a community-led initiative focused on promoting girls' education and empowering young women. There, they met Ms. Phiri, a passionate advocate who spoke about the importance of challenging gender stereotypes and creating a supportive environment for girls to thrive.

Ms. Phiri shared her experiences working with girls in the community, providing mentorship and guidance to help them realize their full potential. She emphasized the need for policies and programs that addressed the root causes of gender inequality and promoted equal rights and opportunities for all.

Inspired by what they had witnessed, Chilufya and his team returned to Kasama, determined to apply the lessons learned to their own community. They organized a meeting under the baobab tree, inviting local leaders, women's rights activists, and community members to join the conversation.

Chilufya shared the success stories from Lusaka and Lundazi, highlighting the importance of promoting gender equality in building a more just and prosperous society. He proposed initiatives such as girls' education programs, women's entrepreneurship initiatives, and gender-sensitive policies that would empower women and challenge gender norms.

One of the local activists, Mrs. Mutale, shared her experience advocating for women's rights in Kasama and the need for policies that addressed the unique challenges faced by women in the community. "By promoting gender equality, we can unlock the potential of half of our population and create a more inclusive and equitable society," she said.

The villagers expressed their support for the proposed initiatives, recognizing the importance of empowering women as agents of change in their community. They discussed ways to challenge gender stereotypes, increase women's representation in leadership roles, and ensure equal access to resources and opportunities for all members of society.

The local councilors pledged their support, promising to enact policies and allocate resources to promote gender equality in Kasama. They agreed to work closely with women's rights activists and community organizations to implement these initiatives and create a more inclusive and equitable community for all.

As the stars twinkled overhead, casting a soft glow over the village, Chilufya stood before the gathered community. "We have learned that by promoting gender equality, we can unlock the full potential of our society and create a future where everyone has the opportunity to thrive," he said. "Let us work together, empowering women and girls, and building a more just and equitable community for all."

With unity, determination, and a commitment to equality, Chilufya and his team felt empowered to lead Kasama towards a future where gender equality was not just a dream, but a reality. They knew that by embracing the principles of social policy and equity, they could create a community where everyone had the chance to live a life of dignity, freedom, and fulfillment.

6

Chapter 6: Infrastructure and Transportation

Infrastructure Investment and Planning

"Paths of Progress"

Beneath the sprawling branches of the ancient baobab tree, the villagers of Kasama gathered once more, their faces alight with anticipation. Today, Chilufya and his team embarked on a journey through the transformative landscape of infrastructure and transportation—a vital cornerstone of progress and development. With the "Building Better Communities" handbook guiding their way, they delved into the intricacies of infrastructure investment and planning, eager to pave the roads to a brighter future for their community.

Chilufya took center stage, his voice resonating through the gathering as he emphasized the pivotal role of infrastructure in shaping the destiny of their village. He spoke of roads connecting distant corners, bridges spanning rivers, and power lines illuminating the night—a symphony of progress echoing through time.

To ground their understanding in reality, Chilufya and his team set out to explore the arteries of development coursing through Zambia. Their first stop was the bustling town of Kabwe, where they hoped to learn from the architects of progress shaping the landscape.

In Kabwe, they were greeted by Mr. Mwamba, a seasoned engineer with a vision as vast as the horizon. He led them through the maze of construction sites and blueprints, where the dreams of a better tomorrow took shape in concrete and steel.

As they traversed the city, Chilufya and his team marveled at the intricate dance of cranes and bulldozers, the symphony of progress reverberating in every beam and rivet. Mr. Mwamba spoke of the importance of strategic planning, of foresight and vision guiding the hand of progress.

Next, the team journeyed to the rural heartlands of Mongu, where the rhythms of life flowed with the tranquil waters of the Zambezi. There, they met with Ms. Namukwai, a community leader with a passion for progress rooted in the soil of her ancestors.

Ms. Namukwai shared tales of bridges spanning chasms, of roads carving paths through the wilderness, and of solar panels whispering secrets to the wind. She spoke of the transformative power of infrastructure investment, of how it breathed life into dreams and prosperity into the land.

Inspired by what they had witnessed, Chilufya and his team returned to Kasama, their hearts ablaze with the fire of possibility. They convened a meeting under the baobab tree, inviting the elders, the visionaries, and the dreamers to join them on their journey.

Chilufya shared the stories of Kabwe and Mongu, of the tireless hands shaping the destiny of their communities. He spoke of the importance of strategic planning, of investment that reached beyond the horizon to embrace the dreams of generations yet unborn.

One of the local elders, Mr. Bwalya, spoke of the dreams of his youth—of roads that led to distant horizons, of bridges that spanned the divide between past and future. "By investing in infrastructure, we pave the way to progress," he declared, his voice resonating with the wisdom of ages.

The villagers nodded in agreement, their eyes alight with the fire of possibility. They spoke of roads that would connect distant villages, of bridges that would span the rivers of time, of power lines that would illuminate the darkness of the night.

The local councilors pledged their support, promising to invest in infrastructure that would lay the foundation for a brighter future for Kasama. They agreed to work hand in hand with the community, ensuring that every road led not just to progress, but to prosperity and opportunity for all.

As the sun dipped below the horizon, casting a golden glow over the village, Chilufya stood before the gathered multitude. "We have learned that by investing in infrastructure, we pave the paths to progress," he declared, his voice echoing through the ages. "Let us embark on this journey together, with courage and determination, knowing that every road we build leads to a brighter tomorrow."

With unity in their hearts and purpose in their steps, Chilufya and his team set forth, their eyes fixed on the distant horizon where the dreams of a better tomorrow awaited. They knew that with every road they paved, they were not just building infrastructure, but forging the paths of progress for generations to come.

Public Transportation Policies

"Journeys of Connectivity"

Under the vast expanse of the baobab tree, amidst the whispers of the wind and the rustle of leaves, the villagers of Kasama gathered once again. Today, Chilufya and his team continued their exploration of infrastructure and transportation, focusing on the vital arteries of public transportation policies. With the "Building Better Communities" handbook as their compass, they embarked on a journey to understand how connectivity through public transportation could weave together the fabric of their community.

Chilufya's voice carried across the gathering, echoing with a resonance that seemed to stir the very roots of the ancient tree. He spoke of the importance of public transportation policies, of how they were the lifelines that connected communities, linked dreams, and bridged divides.

To delve deeper into this realm of connectivity, Chilufya and his team set forth on a voyage across Zambia. Their first destination was the vibrant city of Kitwe, where the pulse of urban life beat in rhythm with the trundle of wheels on pavement.

In Kitwe, they were welcomed by Mr. Chanda, a transport planner with a vision as vast as the sprawling cityscape. He guided them through the bustling streets, where buses and taxis weaved through the traffic like threads in a tapestry.

As they navigated the maze of urban arteries, Chilufya and his team marveled at the intricate dance of commuters and vehicles, the heartbeat of the city pulsating in every honk and hustle. Mr. Chanda spoke of the importance of public transportation in fostering mobility, accessibility, and inclusivity in urban centers.

Next, the team journeyed to the rural hinterlands of Chinsali, where the rhythms of life flowed with the gentle cadence of nature. There, they met with Ms. Bwalya, a community leader with a passion for connectivity that reached beyond the boundaries of her village.

Ms. Bwalya shared tales of dusty roads and long journeys, of buses that arrived once in a blue moon, and of the dreams that slipped through the cracks of time. She spoke of the transformative power of public transportation in connecting rural communities to opportunities, services, and each other.

Inspired by what they had witnessed, Chilufya and his team returned to Kasama, their hearts ablaze with the fire of possibility. They convened a meeting under the baobab tree, inviting the commuters, the dreamers, and the visionaries to join them on their journey.

Chilufya shared the stories of Kitwe and Chinsali, of the arteries of connectivity that pulsated through the veins of urban centers and rural landscapes alike. He spoke of the importance of public transportation policies that prioritized accessibility, affordability, and sustainability for all members of society.

One of the local commuters, Ms. Mulenga, spoke of the journeys she had taken, of the struggles she had faced, and of the dreams she had dared to dream. "By investing in public transportation, we pave the pathways to opportunity for all," she declared, her voice carrying the hopes of a thousand travelers.

The villagers nodded in agreement, their eyes alight with the fire of possibility. They spoke of buses that would ply the dusty roads, of taxis that would crisscross the city streets, of trains that would chug through the countryside, connecting hearts and minds across the land.

The local councilors pledged their support, promising to invest in public transportation policies that would lay the tracks of connectivity for Kasama. They agreed to work hand in hand with the community, ensuring that every journey led not just to a destination, but to a brighter future for all.

As the stars twinkled overhead, casting a shimmering glow over the village, Chilufya stood before the gathered multitude. "We have learned that by investing in public transportation, we pave the pathways to connectivity and opportunity," he declared, his voice echoing through the night. "Let us embark on this journey together, with courage and determination, knowing that every journey we take brings us one step closer to a better tomorrow."

With unity in their hearts and purpose in their steps, Chilufya and his team set forth, their eyes fixed on the distant horizon where the dreams of a connected community awaited. They knew that with every policy they crafted, every road they paved, and every journey they undertook, they were not just building infrastructure but forging the pathways to a future of unity, accessibility, and opportunity for all.

Sustainable Urban Development

"Harmony in Progress"

Beneath the overarching branches of the age-old baobab tree, the villagers of Kasama gathered once more, their anticipation palpable in the gentle breeze that swept through the gathering. Today, Chilufya and his team continued their exploration of infrastructure and transportation, delving into the realm of sustainable urban development—a vision of progress in harmony with nature. With the "Building Better Communities" handbook as their guide, they embarked on a journey to understand how sustainable practices could shape the future of their community.

Chilufya's voice resonated with a sense of purpose as he addressed the assembly, emphasizing the critical importance of sustainable urban development in shaping the destiny of their village. He spoke of the need to create cities and towns that thrived in harmony with nature, where progress walked hand in hand with environmental stewardship.

To immerse themselves in the principles of sustainable urban development, Chilufya and his team set forth on a journey across Zambia. Their first stop was the bustling metropolis of Lusaka, where the heartbeat of urban life pulsed with the rhythm of progress.

In Lusaka, they were greeted by Ms. Ngoma, an urban planner with a vision as vast as the horizon that stretched before them. She led them through the streets, where skyscrapers reached for the sky and green spaces offered respite from the hustle and bustle of city life.

As they navigated the urban landscape, Chilufya and his team marveled at the seamless integration of nature and infrastructure, the symphony of progress echoing in every park and plaza. Ms. Ngoma spoke of the importance of sustainable practices in urban planning, from green building designs to efficient waste management systems.

Next, the team journeyed to the rural town of Mansa, where the rhythms of life flowed with the gentle cadence of the land. There, they met with Mr. Banda, a community leader with a passion for sustainability that ran as deep as the roots of the ancient trees that surrounded them.

Mr. Banda shared tales of sustainable farming practices, of renewable energy projects, and of the dreams of a community living in harmony with nature. He spoke of the transformative power of sustainable urban development in creating cities and towns that nourished both the body and the soul.

Inspired by what they had witnessed, Chilufya and his team returned to Kasama, their hearts ablaze with the fire of possibility. They convened a meeting under the baobab tree, inviting the visionaries, the environmentalists, and the dreamers to join them on their journey.

Chilufya shared the stories of Lusaka and Mansa, of the cities and towns that had embraced the principles of sustainability in their quest for progress. He spoke of the importance of sustainable urban development in creating communities that were resilient, vibrant, and inclusive for all.

One of the local environmentalists, Ms. Mulenga, spoke of the importance of preserving the natural beauty of Kasama while embracing progress. "By investing in sustainable urban development, we can create cities and towns that are not just places to live, but places to thrive," she declared, her voice carrying the hopes of a greener tomorrow.

The villagers nodded in agreement, their eyes alight with the fire of possibility. They spoke of parks that would echo with the laughter of children, of streets lined with trees that whispered secrets to the wind, of buildings that would breathe life into the urban landscape.

The local councilors pledged their support, promising to invest in sustainable urban development policies that would lay the foundations for a greener, more prosperous future for Kasama. They agreed to work hand in hand with the community, ensuring that every step they took toward progress was a step toward harmony with nature.

As the sun dipped below the horizon, casting a golden glow over the village, Chilufya stood before the gathered multitude. "We have learned that by embracing sustainable urban development, we can create communities that thrive in harmony with nature," he declared, his voice echoing through the gathering. "Let us embark on this journey together, with courage and determination, knowing that every step we take toward progress is a step toward a brighter, greener future."

With unity in their hearts and purpose in their steps, Chilufya and his team set forth, their eyes fixed on the horizon where the dreams of a sustainable community awaited. They knew that with every policy they crafted, every building they designed, and every park they planted, they were not just building infrastructure but forging a future where progress and nature walked hand in hand.

Digital Infrastructure and Connectivity

"Bridging the Digital Divide"

Underneath the expansive canopy of the ancient baobab tree, the villagers of Kasama gathered once more, their faces alight with anticipation. Today, Chilufya and his team delved further into the realm of infrastructure and transportation, focusing on the transformative power of digital infrastructure and connectivity—a gateway to knowledge, opportunity, and progress. With the "Building Better Communities" handbook as their compass, they embarked on a journey to understand how digital technologies could bridge the gap and pave the way for a more connected future.

Chilufya's voice carried through the gathering, resonating with the promise of a future illuminated by the glow of digital connectivity. He spoke of the transformative impact of digital infrastructure in unlocking the vast reservoirs of knowledge, innovation, and opportunity that lay beyond the horizon.

To immerse themselves in the world of digital connectivity, Chilufya and his team embarked on a journey across Zambia. Their first destination was the bustling city of Ndola, where the hum of technology reverberated in the air, and the pulse of progress beat in rhythm with the click of keyboards.

In Ndola, they were greeted by Mr. Sichone, a digital strategist with a vision as vast as the endless streams of data that flowed through the city. He led them through the bustling streets, where digital billboards blinked with messages of possibility and promise.

As they navigated the digital landscape, Chilufya and his team marveled at the seamless integration of technology into every facet of urban life, from smart grids to e-government services. Mr. Sichone spoke of the importance of digital infrastructure in driving economic growth, enhancing public services, and empowering communities to thrive in the digital age.

Next, the team journeyed to the remote village of Choma, where the rhythms of life flowed with the gentle cadence of tradition. There, they met with Ms. Masinja, a community leader with a passion for harnessing the power of technology to transform lives.

Ms. Masinja shared tales of connectivity bridging the gap between urban centers and rural communities, of mobile phones unlocking access to education, healthcare, and economic opportunity. She spoke of the transformative power of digital connectivity in leveling the playing field and empowering individuals to realize their full potential.

Inspired by what they had witnessed, Chilufya and his team returned to Kasama, their hearts ablaze with the fire of possibility. They convened a meeting under the baobab tree, inviting the tech enthusiasts, the entrepreneurs, and the dreamers to join them on their journey.

Chilufya shared the stories of Ndola and Choma, of the cities and villages that had embraced the digital revolution in their quest for progress. He spoke of the importance of digital infrastructure in connecting communities, fostering innovation, and driving sustainable development.

One of the local entrepreneurs, Mr. Bwalya, spoke of the transformative impact of digital connectivity on his business and his community. "By investing in digital infrastructure, we can unlock new opportunities, new markets, and new possibilities for growth," he declared, his voice filled with the optimism of a brighter tomorrow.

The villagers nodded in agreement, their eyes alight with

the fire of possibility. They spoke of schools equipped with computers, of clinics connected to telemedicine services, of businesses reaching customers across the globe with the click of a button.

The local councilors pledged their support, promising to invest in digital infrastructure policies that would lay the foundation for a more connected, more prosperous future for Kasama. They agreed to work hand in hand with the community, ensuring that every step they took toward digital progress was a step toward inclusivity, accessibility, and opportunity for all.

As the stars twinkled overhead, casting a shimmering glow over the village, Chilufya stood before the gathered multitude. "We have learned that by embracing digital infrastructure and connectivity, we can create communities that thrive in the digital age," he declared, his voice echoing through the gathering. "Let us embark on this journey together, with courage and determination, knowing that every step we take toward digital progress is a step toward a brighter, more connected future."

With unity in their hearts and purpose in their steps, Chilufya and his team set forth, their eyes fixed on the horizon where the dreams of a connected community awaited. They knew that with every policy they crafted, every fiber optic cable they laid, and every Wi-Fi hotspot they installed, they were not just building infrastructure but forging a future where connectivity was not a luxury but a fundamental right for all.

Energy Policy and Sustainability

"Energizing Tomorrow"

Beneath the sprawling branches of the ancient baobab tree, the villagers of Kasama gathered once more, their anticipation palpable in the gentle breeze that rustled through the leaves. Today, Chilufya and his team continued their exploration of infrastructure and transportation, delving into the realm of energy policy and sustainability—a beacon of hope for a future powered by renewable resources and environmental stewardship. With the "Building Better Communities" handbook guiding their path, they embarked on a journey to understand how sustainable energy practices could light the way to a brighter tomorrow.

Chilufya's voice rang out with a sense of purpose as he addressed the gathering, emphasizing the critical importance of energy policy and sustainability in shaping the destiny of their village. He spoke of the need to harness the power of renewable resources to fuel their community's progress while preserving the delicate balance of their natural environment.

To immerse themselves in the realm of sustainable energy, Chilufya and his team set forth on a journey across Zambia. Their first destination was the bustling city of Livingstone, where the roar of Victoria Falls echoed in the air, and the promise of hydroelectric power filled the horizon.

In Livingstone, they were greeted by Mr. Mwale, an energy expert with a vision as vast as the cascading waters that surrounded them. He led them through the bustling streets, where solar panels glistened under the African sun, and wind turbines spun gracefully in the breeze.

As they navigated the landscape of renewable energy, Chilufya and his team marveled at the ingenuity of human innovation, the symphony of progress reverberating in every ray of sunlight and gust of wind. Mr. Mwale spoke of the importance of sustainable energy practices in reducing carbon emissions, mitigating climate change, and securing a brighter future for generations to come.

Next, the team journeyed to the rural heartlands of Choma, where the rhythms of life flowed with the gentle cadence of the land. There, they met with Ms. Mulenga, a community leader with a passion for sustainability that ran as deep as the roots of the ancient trees that surrounded them.

Ms. Mulenga shared tales of solar panels powering homes, of biogas digesters turning waste into energy, and of the dreams of a community living in harmony with nature. She spoke of the transformative power of sustainable energy in fostering resilience, self-reliance, and prosperity for all.

Inspired by what they had witnessed, Chilufya and his team returned to Kasama, their hearts ablaze with the fire of possibility. They convened a meeting under the baobab tree, inviting the environmentalists, the engineers, and the dreamers to join them on their journey.

Chilufya shared the stories of Livingstone and Choma, of the cities and villages that had embraced sustainable energy practices in their quest for progress. He spoke of the importance of energy policy and sustainability in safeguarding their community's future while unlocking new opportunities for growth and development.

One of the local engineers, Mr. Bwalya, spoke of the transformative impact of sustainable energy on his community's resilience and prosperity. "By investing in renewable resources, we can secure a brighter future for ourselves and our children," he declared, his voice filled with the optimism of a community energized by possibility.

The villagers nodded in agreement, their eyes alight with the fire of possibility. They spoke of homes powered by sunlight, of farms irrigated by wind, of industries fueled by the energy of their own innovation.

The local councilors pledged their support, promising to invest in energy policies and sustainability initiatives that would lay the foundation for a more resilient, more prosperous future for Kasama. They agreed to work hand in hand with the community, ensuring that every step they took toward sustainable energy was a step toward environmental stewardship and economic empowerment for all.

As the sun dipped below the horizon, casting a golden glow over the village, Chilufya stood before the gathered multitude. "We have learned that by embracing sustainable energy practices, we can create communities that thrive in harmony with nature," he declared, his voice echoing through the gathering. "Let us embark on this journey together, with courage and determination, knowing that every step we take toward sustainable energy is a step toward a brighter, more resilient future."

With unity in their hearts and purpose in their steps, Chilufya and his team set forth, their eyes fixed on the horizon where the dreams of an energy-rich, environmentally sustainable community awaited. They knew that with every policy they crafted, every renewable resource they harnessed, and every environmental challenge they tackled, they were not just building infrastructure but forging a future where energy flowed freely, sustainably, and equitably for all.

Disaster Preparedness and Resilience

"Rising from the Ashes"

Underneath the sprawling branches of the ancient baobab tree, the villagers of Kasama gathered once more, their faces etched with determination. Today, Chilufya and his team delved deeper into the realm of infrastructure and transportation, focusing on disaster preparedness and resilience—a beacon of hope in the face of adversity. With the "Building Better Communities" handbook as their guiding light, they embarked on a journey to understand how to fortify their community against the ravages of nature.

Chilufya's voice cut through the stillness of the gathering, carrying with it a sense of urgency and resolve. He spoke of the importance of disaster preparedness and resilience, of the need to fortify their community against the wrath of nature's fury.

To delve deeper into this realm of fortitude, Chilufya and his team embarked on a journey across Zambia. Their first stop was the coastal town of Livingstone, where the mighty Zambezi River flowed majestically into the horizon.

In Livingstone, they were greeted by Mr. Sichone, a disaster management expert with a steely resolve born from years of battling nature's wrath. He led them through the bustling streets, where flood barriers stood sentinel against the rising tide, and evacuation routes were marked with clarity.

As they navigated the landscape of disaster preparedness, Chilufya and his team marveled at the meticulous planning and foresight that went into safeguarding the town against calamity. Mr. Sichone spoke of the importance of early warning systems, emergency shelters, and community resilience in the face of disaster.

Next, the team journeyed to the rural heartlands of Choma, where the rhythms of life flowed with the gentle cadence of the land. There, they met with Ms. Masinja, a community leader with a spirit as indomitable as the winds that swept across the plains.

Ms. Masinja shared tales of drought and famine, of floods and landslides, and of the resilience of her people in the face of adversity. She spoke of the importance of community cohesion, of neighbors helping neighbors, and of the bonds that held them together in times of crisis.

Inspired by what they had witnessed, Chilufya and his team returned to Kasama, their hearts heavy with the weight of responsibility. They convened a meeting under the baobab tree, inviting the elders, the leaders, and the guardians of their community to join them on their journey.

Chilufya shared the stories of Livingstone and Choma, of the towns and villages that had weathered the storms of nature with courage and resilience. He spoke of the importance of disaster preparedness and resilience in safeguarding their community's future and protecting the lives and livelihoods of its inhabitants.

One of the local elders, Mr. Bwalya, spoke of the lessons learned from past disasters and the need to heed nature's warnings. "By investing in disaster preparedness and resilience, we can ensure that our community rises from the ashes stronger and more united than ever before," he declared, his voice echoing with the wisdom of ages.

The villagers nodded in agreement, their eyes alight with the fire of determination. They spoke of building stronger homes, of planting resilient crops, and of coming together as a community to face whatever challenges lay ahead.

The local councilors pledged their support, promising to invest in disaster preparedness and resilience initiatives that would lay the foundation for a more secure and prosperous future for Kasama. They agreed to work hand in hand with the community, ensuring that every step they took toward resilience was a step toward safety and security for all.

As the sun dipped below the horizon, casting a golden glow over the village, Chilufya stood before the gathered multitude. "We have learned that by embracing disaster preparedness and resilience, we can build a community that is strong, united, and unyielding in the face of adversity," he declared, his voice ringing with conviction. "Let us embark on this journey together, with courage and determination, knowing that every step we take toward resilience is a step toward a brighter, more secure future."

With unity in their hearts and purpose in their steps, Chilufya and his team set forth, their eyes fixed on the horizon where the dreams of a resilient community awaited. They knew that with every policy they crafted, every evacuation route they mapped, and every community bond they forged, they were not just building infrastructure but fortifying the spirit of their community against whatever challenges the future may hold.

7

Chapter 7: Environmental Policy and Sustainability

Climate Change Mitigation and Adaptation Strategies

"Guardians of the Earth"

Amidst the ancient baobab trees, their branches reaching towards the sky like ancient sentinels, the villagers of Kasama gathered once more. Today, Chilufya and his team embarked on a journey into the heart of environmental policy and sustainability, seeking ways to protect their beloved land from the ravages of climate change. With the "Building Better Communities" handbook as their guide, they set out to understand how mitigation and adaptation strategies could safeguard their community for generations to come.

Chilufya's voice cut through the stillness of the gathering, carrying with it a sense of urgency and determination. He spoke of the looming threat of climate change, of the rising temperatures, erratic weather patterns, and encroaching desertification that threatened their way of life.

To confront this existential challenge, Chilufya and his team embarked on a journey across Zambia. Their first destination was the lush forests of Kasanka National Park, where the symphony of nature echoed through the canopy, and the whispers of the wind carried tales of resilience and adaptation.

In Kasanka, they were greeted by Ms. Mwape, a conservationist with a passion as deep as the roots of the ancient trees that surrounded them. She led them through the verdant landscape, where elephants roamed freely and birdsong filled the air.

As they immersed themselves in the natural splendor of the park, Chilufya and his team marveled at the intricate web of life that thrived despite the challenges of a changing climate. Ms. Mwape spoke of the importance of conservation efforts in protecting biodiversity, preserving ecosystems, and mitigating the impacts of climate change.

Next, the team journeyed to the arid plains of Kafue, where the rhythms of life flowed with the gentle cadence of the land. There, they met with Mr. Musonda, a farmer with a spirit as indomitable as the sun that beat down upon the parched earth.

Mr. Musonda shared tales of drought and famine, of crops withering in the relentless heat, and of the resilience of his community in the face of adversity. He spoke of the importance of adaptation strategies, from drought-resistant crops to water conservation techniques, in building resilience and ensuring food security in a changing climate.

Inspired by what they had witnessed, Chilufya and his team returned to Kasama, their hearts heavy with the weight of responsibility. They convened a meeting under the baobab tree, inviting the farmers, the conservationists, and the guardians of their land to join them on their journey.

Chilufya shared the stories of Kasanka and Kafue, of the ecosystems and communities that had weathered the storms of climate change with resilience and adaptation. He spoke of the importance of environmental policy and sustainability in safeguarding their community's future and protecting the land they called home.

One of the local conservationists, Ms. Banda, spoke of the urgency of action and the need to confront climate change head-on. "By investing in mitigation and adaptation strategies, we can protect our land, our livelihoods, and our way of life for generations to come," she declared, her voice filled with determination.

The villagers nodded in agreement, their eyes alight with the fire of resolve. They spoke of planting trees to combat deforestation, of conserving water to combat drought, and of coming together as a community to confront the challenges of a changing climate.

The local councilors pledged their support, promising to invest in environmental policy and sustainability initiatives that would lay the foundation for a more resilient and sustainable future for Kasama. They agreed to work hand in hand with the community, ensuring that every step they took toward mitigation and adaptation was a step toward safeguarding their land and their legacy.

As the sun dipped below the horizon, casting a golden glow over the village, Chilufya stood before the gathered multitude. "We have learned that by embracing environmental policy and sustainability, we can protect our land, our livelihoods, and our way of life for generations to come," he declared, his voice ringing with conviction. "Let us embark on this journey together, with courage and determination, knowing that every step we take toward resilience is a step toward a brighter, more sustainable future."

With unity in their hearts and purpose in their steps, Chilufya and his team set forth, their eyes fixed on the horizon where the dreams of a resilient and sustainable community awaited. They knew that with every policy they crafted, every tree they planted, and every drop of water they conserved, they were not just building infrastructure but stewarding the earth and safeguarding their home for generations to come.

Conservation Policies for Natural Resources

"Guardians of the Wild"

Beneath the sprawling branches of the ancient baobab tree, the villagers of Kasama gathered once more, their hearts filled with reverence for the land that sustained them. Today, Chilufya and his team delved deeper into the realm of environmental policy and sustainability, focusing on the crucial role of conservation policies in protecting their precious natural resources. With the "Building Better Communities" handbook as their compass, they embarked on a journey to understand how to preserve the biodiversity and beauty of their land for future generations.

Chilufya's voice resonated with solemnity as he addressed the gathering, emphasizing the sacred duty they bore as stewards of the earth. He spoke of the rich tapestry of life that flourished in their midst, from the towering forests to the winding rivers, and of the urgent need to safeguard these treasures for posterity.

To delve deeper into the realm of conservation, Chilufya and his team embarked on a journey across Zambia. Their first destination was the pristine wilderness of South Luangwa National Park, where the symphony of nature echoed through the savannah, and the majestic wildlife roamed free.

In South Luangwa, they were greeted by Mr. Mwale, a park ranger with a deep love for the land he protected. He led them through the rugged terrain, where elephants trumpeted in the distance, and lions prowled beneath the dappled shade of acacia trees.

As they immersed themselves in the natural splendor of the park, Chilufya and his team marveled at the diversity of life that thrived within its boundaries. Mr. Mwale spoke of the importance of conservation policies in preserving habitats, protecting endangered species, and maintaining the delicate balance of the ecosystem.

Next, the team journeyed to the verdant valleys of Kafue, where the rhythms of life flowed with the gentle cadence of the land. There, they met with Ms. Masinja, a farmer with a deep respect for the land that sustained her.

Ms. Masinja shared tales of the bountiful harvests that flourished in harmony with nature, of the rivers that teemed with life, and of the wisdom passed down through generations. She spoke of the importance of sustainable agriculture practices, of land use policies that respected the earth's finite resources, and of the need to strike a balance between progress and preservation.

Inspired by what they had witnessed, Chilufya and his team returned to Kasama, their hearts heavy with the weight of responsibility. They convened a meeting under the baobab tree, inviting the farmers, the rangers, and the guardians of their land to join them on their journey.

Chilufya shared the stories of South Luangwa and Kafue, of the protected areas and sustainable farms that had thrived under the watchful eye of conservation policies. He spoke of the importance of environmental policy and sustainability in safeguarding their community's future and protecting the natural resources they depended upon.

One of the local farmers, Mr. Bwalya, spoke of the interconnectedness of all life and the need to protect the land that sustained them. "By investing in conservation policies, we can ensure that our children inherit a world rich in biodiversity and beauty," he declared, his voice filled with conviction.

The villagers nodded in agreement, their eyes alight with the fire of determination. They spoke of preserving forests and wetlands, of protecting endangered species, and of coming together as a community to safeguard the earth that nourished them.

The local councilors pledged their support, promising to invest in conservation policies and sustainable land management practices that would lay the foundation for a more resilient and biodiverse future for Kasama. They agreed to work hand in hand with the community, ensuring that every step they took toward conservation was a step toward preserving their natural heritage for generations to come.

As the sun dipped below the horizon, casting a golden glow over the village, Chilufya stood before the gathered multitude. "We have learned that by embracing conservation policies, we can protect our precious natural resources and safeguard the biodiversity of our land," he declared, his voice ringing with conviction. "Let us embark on this journey together, with courage and determination, knowing that every step we take toward conservation is a step toward a brighter, more sustainable future."

With unity in their hearts and purpose in their steps, Chilufya and his team set forth, their eyes fixed on the horizon where the dreams of a biodiverse and resilient community awaited. They knew that with every policy they crafted, every habitat they protected, and every species they saved, they were not just building infrastructure but preserving the very essence of life itself.

Biodiversity Protection and Ecosystem Management

"Guardians of the Wild"

Underneath the sprawling branches of the ancient baobab tree, the villagers of Kasama gathered once more, their faces etched with determination. Today, Chilufya and his team continued their exploration of environmental policy and sustainability, delving into the vital realm of biodiversity protection and ecosystem management. With the "Building Better Communities" handbook guiding their path, they embarked on a journey to understand how to safeguard the rich tapestry of life that thrived within their midst.

Chilufya's voice carried through the gathering, resonating with the urgency of their mission. He spoke of the intricate web of life that interconnected their world, from the smallest insect to the mightiest elephant, and of the imperative to protect this biodiversity for the well-being of their community and the planet.

To delve deeper into the realm of biodiversity protection, Chilufya and his team embarked on a journey across Zambia. Their first destination was the lush wetlands of Bangweulu, where the symphony of nature echoed through the reeds, and the shimmering waters teemed with life.

In Bangweulu, they were greeted by Ms. Mwansa, a conservation biologist with a passion as deep as the waters that surrounded them. She led them through the maze of channels and islands, where birds danced in the sky and fish darted beneath the surface.

As they immersed themselves in the natural splendor of the wetlands, Chilufya and his team marveled at the richness of biodiversity that thrived within its boundaries. Ms. Mwansa spoke of the importance of protecting habitats, conserving species, and restoring ecosystems to ensure the resilience of the natural world.

Next, the team journeyed to the lush forests of Kasanka, where the rhythms of life flowed with the gentle cadence of the land. There, they met with Mr. Mulenga, a forest ranger with a reverence for the ancient trees that towered above them.

Mr. Mulenga shared tales of the diverse array of life that called the forest home, from the elusive leopard to the majestic sable antelope. He spoke of the importance of sustainable land management practices, of preserving biodiversity hotspots, and of the need to strike a balance between human needs and the needs of nature.

Inspired by what they had witnessed, Chilufya and his team returned to Kasama, their hearts heavy with the weight of responsibility. They convened a meeting under the baobab tree, inviting the conservationists, the rangers, and the guardians of their land to join them on their journey.

Chilufya shared the stories of Bangweulu and Kasanka, of the wetlands and forests that had thrived under the watchful eye of biodiversity protection and ecosystem management. He spoke of the importance of environmental policy and sustainability in safeguarding their community's future and protecting the natural resources they depended upon.

One of the local rangers, Ms. Banda, spoke of the interconnectedness of all life and the need to protect the delicate balance of ecosystems. "By investing in biodiversity protection and ecosystem management, we can ensure that our planet remains a vibrant and thriving home for all species," she declared, her voice filled with conviction.

The villagers nodded in agreement, their eyes alight with the fire of determination. They spoke of preserving wetlands and forests, of conserving endangered species, and of coming together as a community to safeguard the biodiversity that enriched their lives.

The local councilors pledged their support, promising to invest in conservation policies and sustainable land management practices that would lay the foundation for a more resilient and biodiverse future for Kasama. They agreed to work hand in hand with the community, ensuring that every step they took toward biodiversity protection was a step toward preserving the natural heritage that sustained them.

As the sun dipped below the horizon, casting a golden glow over the village, Chilufya stood before the gathered multitude. "We have learned that by embracing biodiversity protection and ecosystem management Bament, we can safeguard the rich tapestry of life that thrives within our midst," he declared, his voice ringing with conviction. "Let us embark on this journey together, with courage and determination, knowing that every step we take toward conservation is a step toward a brighter, more sustainable future."

With unity in their hearts and purpose in their steps, Chilufya and his team set forth, their eyes fixed on the horizon where the dreams of a biodiverse and resilient community awaited. They knew that with every policy they crafted, every habitat they protected, and every species they saved, they were not just building infrastructure but preserving the very essence of life itself.

Renewable Energy Policies

"Harmony in the Winds"

Amidst the swaying branches of the ancient baobab tree, the villagers of Kasama congregated once more, their gazes focused on Chilufya and his team. Today, their journey through environmental policy and sustainability led them to the crucial realm of renewable energy policies—a path toward harnessing the power of nature to secure a sustainable future. With the "Building Better Communities" handbook as their guide, they embarked on a quest to understand how renewable energy could light the way to a greener, more harmonious world.

Chilufya's voice resonated with hope as he addressed the gathering, emphasizing the transformative potential of renewable energy in their community. He spoke of the winds that whispered through the valleys, the sun that bathed the land in warmth, and the rivers that flowed with untapped power—all waiting to be harnessed for the greater good.

To delve deeper into the realm of renewable energy, Chilufya and his team embarked on a journey across Zambia. Their first destination was the sun-kissed plains of Mongu, where the golden rays danced across fields of sugarcane, and the promise of solar power filled the air.

In Mongu, they were greeted by Mr. Musonda, a solar engineer with a vision as vast as the endless horizon. He led them through the fields, where solar panels gleamed under the African sun, and the hum of renewable energy filled the air.

As they immersed themselves in the brilliance of solar power, Chilufya and his team marveled at the ingenuity of human innovation. Mr. Musonda spoke of the importance of renewable energy policies in reducing carbon emissions, mitigating climate change, and securing a brighter future for generations to come.

Next, the team journeyed to the rugged hills of Mpika, where the rhythms of life flowed with the gentle cadence of the land. There, they met with Ms. Bwalya, a wind energy specialist with a passion as fierce as the gusts that swept across the plains.

Ms. Bwalya shared tales of wind farms that dotted the landscape, their turbines spinning gracefully in the breeze, and the promise of clean, sustainable power that they brought to the community. She spoke of the importance of diversifying their energy sources, of harnessing the power of the wind to create a more resilient and sustainable future.

Inspired by what they had witnessed, Chilufya and his team returned to Kasama, their hearts ablaze with the fire of possibility. They convened a meeting under the baobab tree, inviting the engineers, the innovators, and the dreamers to join them on their journey.

Chilufya shared the stories of Mongu and Mpika, of the towns and villages that had embraced renewable energy policies in their quest for progress. He spoke of the importance of environmental policy and sustainability in safeguarding their community's future while unlocking new opportunities for growth and development.

One of the local innovators, Ms. Mulenga, spoke of the transformative impact of renewable energy on her community's resilience and prosperity. "By investing in renewable energy policies, we can secure a brighter future for ourselves and our children," she declared, her voice filled with the optimism of a community energized by possibility.

The villagers nodded in agreement, their eyes alight with the fire of possibility. They spoke of homes powered by sunlight, of farms irrigated by wind, and of industries fueled by the energy of their own innovation.

The local councilors pledged their support, promising to invest in renewable energy policies and sustainable development initiatives that would lay the foundation for a more resilient, more prosperous future for Kasama. They agreed to work hand in hand with the community, ensuring that every step they took toward renewable energy was a step toward environmental stewardship and economic empowerment for all.

As the sun dipped below the horizon, casting a golden glow over the village, Chilufya stood before the gathered multitude. "We have learned that by embracing renewable energy policies, we can create communities that thrive in harmony with nature," he declared, his voice echoing through the gathering. "Let us embark on this journey together, with courage and determination, knowing that every step we take toward renewable energy is a step toward a brighter, more sustainable future."

With unity in their hearts and purpose in their steps, Chilufya and his team set forth, their eyes fixed on the horizon where the dreams of an energy-rich, environmentally sustainable community awaited. They knew that with every policy they crafted, every renewable resource they harnessed, and every environmental challenge they tackled, they were not just building infrastructure but forging a future where energy flowed freely, sustainably, and equitably for all.

Pollution Control and Waste Management

"Guardians of Clean Horizons"

Beneath the broad canopy of the ancient baobab tree, the villagers of Kasama gathered once more, their eyes reflecting a shared determination. Today, Chilufya and his team delved deeper into the intricate realm of environmental policy and sustainability, focusing on the urgent need for pollution control and waste management strategies. With the "Building Better Communities" handbook as their compass, they embarked on a journey to cleanse their land and waterways, ensuring a healthier future for all.

Chilufya's voice reverberated with resolve as he addressed the assembly, emphasizing the critical importance of tackling pollution and managing waste for the well-being of their community and the planet. He spoke of the rivers choked with plastic, the air heavy with pollutants, and the imperative to act swiftly and decisively to restore balance to their environment.

To delve deeper into the realm of pollution control and waste management, Chilufya and his team embarked on a journey across Zambia. Their first destination was the bustling city of Lusaka, where the clamor of urban life masked the hidden dangers lurking in the air and water.

In Lusaka, they were greeted by Dr. Kabwe, an environmental scientist with a passion for clean air and water. She led them through the streets, where factories belched smoke into the sky, and rivers ran murky with untreated sewage.

As they navigated the urban landscape, Chilufya and his team were struck by the stark reality of pollution's toll on human health and the environment. Dr. Kabwe spoke of the importance of pollution control measures, from stricter emissions standards to improved waste management practices, in safeguarding public health and restoring ecological balance.

Next, the team journeyed to the tranquil shores of Lake Tanganyika, where the rhythms of life flowed with the gentle cadence of the waves. There, they met with Mr. Ngoma, a fisherman with a love for the pristine waters that sustained his livelihood.

Mr. Ngoma shared tales of the lake's once-teeming bounty, now threatened by pollution from industrial runoff and untreated sewage. He spoke of the urgent need for waste management strategies, from recycling initiatives to community clean-up efforts, in preserving the lake's fragile ecosystem and the way of life it supported.

Inspired by what they had witnessed, Chilufya and his team returned to Kasama, their hearts heavy with the weight of responsibility. They convened a meeting under the baobab tree, inviting the environmentalists, the activists, and the guardians of their land to join them on their journey.

Chilufya shared the stories of Lusaka and Lake Tanganyika, of the cities and natural wonders that had fallen victim to pollution's scourge. He spoke of the importance of environmental policy and sustainability in safeguarding their community's health and prosperity while preserving the beauty of their land for future generations.

One of the local activists, Ms. Banda, spoke of the transformative power of collective action and the need to hold polluters accountable. "By investing in pollution control and waste management, we can reclaim our land and waterways from the grip of pollution," she declared, her voice ringing with determination.

The villagers nodded in agreement, their eyes alight with the fire of resolve. They spoke of cleaner air to breathe, of purer water to drink, and of a land free from the blight of pollution.

The local councilors pledged their support, promising to invest in pollution control measures and waste management initiatives that would lay the foundation for a cleaner, healthier future for Kasama. They agreed to work hand in hand with the community, ensuring that every step they took toward pollution control and waste management was a step toward reclaiming their environment and their well-being.

As the sun dipped below the horizon, casting a golden glow over the village, Chilufya stood before the gathered multitude. "We have learned that by embracing pollution control and waste management, we can reclaim our land and waterways from the grip of pollution," he declared, his voice ringing with conviction. "Let us embark on this journey together, with courage and determination, knowing that every step we take toward environmental stewardship is a step toward a cleaner, healthier future."

With unity in their hearts and purpose in their steps, Chilufya and his team set forth, their eyes fixed on the horizon where the dreams of clean air, pure water, and untainted land awaited. They knew that with every policy they crafted, every waste they managed, and every pollutant they curtailed, they were not just building infrastructure but reclaiming their environment and their future from the ravages of pollution.

International Cooperation on Environmental Issues

"Bridging Borders, Sustaining Souls"

Underneath the shade of the ancient baobab tree, the villagers of Kasama assembled once more, their hearts pulsing with a shared commitment. Today, Chilufya and his team journeyed deeper into the realms of environmental policy and sustainability, focusing on the imperative of international cooperation to address global environmental challenges. With the "Building Better Communities" handbook as their beacon, they embarked on a quest to forge bonds across borders, uniting with distant allies in a shared mission to safeguard the planet.

Chilufya's voice rang out with conviction as he addressed the gathering, highlighting the interconnectedness of their world and the necessity of collaboration on a global scale. He spoke of the rivers that flowed across borders, the air currents that knew no boundaries, and the imperative to work hand in hand with neighboring nations to confront environmental threats.

To explore the realm of international cooperation, Chilufya

and his team embarked on a journey that traversed borders and spanned continents. Their first destination was the bustling metropolis of Nairobi, where diplomats and environmentalists converged from around the world to address the pressing issues facing the planet.

In Nairobi, they were greeted by Dr. Amina, a diplomat with a vision as broad as the African savannah. She led them through the corridors of power, where negotiations unfolded amidst the backdrop of looming environmental crises.

As they immersed themselves in the complexities of international diplomacy, Chilufya and his team gained a deeper understanding of the power of collaboration in tackling global challenges. Dr. Amina spoke of the importance of multilateral agreements, from climate accords to biodiversity treaties, in fostering cooperation and driving progress toward a sustainable future.

Next, the team journeyed to the remote reaches of the Amazon rainforest, where the rhythms of life pulsed with primal energy. There, they met with Chief Tupa, a tribal leader with a reverence for the natural world that transcended borders.

Chief Tupa shared tales of the ancient forests that sustained his people for generations, now threatened by deforestation and exploitation. He spoke of the need for solidarity among nations, of recognizing the intrinsic value of nature, and of forging partnerships that honored the sacred bond between humanity and the earth.

Inspired by what they had witnessed, Chilufya and his team returned to Kasama, their hearts brimming with a newfound sense of purpose. They convened a meeting under the baobab tree, inviting leaders from neighboring communities and countries to join them in their quest for environmental stewardship.

Chilufya shared the stories of Nairobi and the Amazon, of the corridors of power and the depths of the rainforest, illustrating the power of collaboration in confronting environmental challenges. He spoke of the importance of environmental policy and sustainability in transcending borders and fostering unity among nations in the pursuit of a shared future.

One of the visiting diplomats, Mr. Kimani, spoke of the transformative potential of international cooperation and the need to bridge divides for the collective good. "By working together across borders, we can harness our collective strength to confront environmental threats and secure a sustainable future for all," he declared, his voice resonating with hope.

The villagers nodded in agreement, their eyes alight with the fire of solidarity. They spoke of building bridges, not walls, of finding common ground, and of forging alliances that transcended politics and geography in the pursuit of environmental harmony.

The visiting leaders pledged their support, promising to collaborate with Kasama and its neighbors on initiatives that would lay the foundation for a more sustainable, more resilient future for all. They agreed to work hand in hand with the community, ensuring that every step they took toward international cooperation was a step toward safeguarding the planet and its inhabitants for generations to come.

As the sun dipped below the horizon, casting a golden glow over the village, Chilufya stood before the gathered multitude. "We have learned that by embracing international cooperation, we can transcend borders and forge a path toward a sustainable future for all," he declared, his voice echoing through the gathering. "Let us embark on this journey together, with courage and determination, knowing that every step we take toward unity is a step toward environmental harmony."

With unity in their hearts and purpose in their steps, Chilufya and his team set forth, their eyes fixed on the horizon where the dreams of a world united in environmental stewardship awaited. They knew that with every policy they crafted, every alliance they forged, and every hand they clasped across borders, they were not just building infrastructure but laying the groundwork for a future where humanity and nature thrived in harmony.

8

Chapter 8: Healthcare Policy and Public Health

Access to Healthcare Services

"Healing Hands, United Hearts"

Beneath the comforting shade of the ancient baobab tree, the villagers of Kasama gathered once more, their faces etched with concern and hope. Today, Chilufya and his team ventured into the realm of healthcare policy and public health, focusing on the fundamental need for access to healthcare services—a lifeline that could mean the difference between life and death. With the "Building Better Communities" handbook guiding their path, they embarked on a journey to ensure that every member of their community had the care they deserved.

Chilufya's voice carried on the gentle breeze as he addressed the gathering, emphasizing the inherent right of every individual to quality healthcare. He spoke of the mothers who suffered in silence, the children who fought against illness, and the imperative to build a healthcare system that reached every corner of their community.

To explore the realm of access to healthcare services, Chilufya and his team ventured across the landscape of Zambia, their hearts heavy with the stories of those who had struggled to access care. Their first destination was the bustling city of Lusaka, where the hospitals overflowed with patients seeking solace amidst the chaos of illness.

In Lusaka, they were greeted by Dr. Mwamba, a tireless physician with a heart as vast as the savannah. She led them through the corridors of the hospital, where the sick lay waiting for care that often arrived too late.

As they navigated the labyrinth of healthcare provision, Chilufya and his team gained a deeper understanding of the barriers that stood between their community and the care they so desperately needed. Dr. Mwamba spoke of the importance of healthcare policy in ensuring equitable access to services, from the remote villages to the bustling cities, and of the need to address systemic inequalities that left so many behind.

Next, the team journeyed to the remote reaches of Western Province, where the rhythms of life flowed with the gentle cadence of the Zambezi River. There, they met with Nurse Kabwe, a dedicated healthcare worker with a spirit as indomitable as the river itself.

Nurse Kabwe shared tales of the challenges she faced in reaching those in need, from the isolated villages nestled along the riverbanks to the nomadic herders who roamed the plains. She spoke of the importance of community health initiatives, of bringing care to the people where they lived, and of the need for policy reforms that recognized the unique needs of rural populations.

Inspired by what they had witnessed, Chilufya and his team returned to Kasama, their hearts heavy with the weight of responsibility. They convened a meeting under the baobab tree, inviting healthcare workers, policymakers, and community leaders to join them on their journey to ensure access to healthcare for all.

Chilufya shared the stories of Lusaka and Western Province, of the hospitals and the remote villages, illustrating the urgent need for healthcare policy reforms that would break down barriers and bring care to those who needed it most. He spoke of the importance of healthcare policy and public health in safeguarding their community's well-being and ensuring that no one was left behind.

One of the local nurses, Ms. Banda, spoke of the transformative power of access to healthcare and the need to prioritize the most vulnerable in their community. "By investing in healthcare policy reforms, we can ensure that every member of our community has access to the care they need to thrive," she declared, her voice filled with determination.

The villagers nodded in agreement, their eyes alight with the fire of solidarity. They spoke of building a healthcare system that left no one behind, of reaching the unreachable, and of ensuring that every member of their community had the chance to live a healthy, fulfilling life.

The local councilors pledged their support, promising to invest in healthcare policy reforms and community health initiatives that would lay the foundation for a more equitable, more resilient future for Kasama. They agreed to work hand in hand with the community, ensuring that every step they took toward access to healthcare services was a step toward healing and hope for all.

As the sun dipped below the horizon, casting a golden glow over the village, Chilufya stood before the gathered multitude. "We have learned that by embracing healthcare policy and public health, we can ensure that every member of our community has access to the care they need to thrive," he declared, his voice echoing through the gathering. "Let us embark on this journey together, with compassion and determination, knowing that every step we take toward access to healthcare services is a step toward a healthier, more vibrant future."

With unity in their hearts and purpose in their steps, Chilufya and his team set forth, their eyes fixed on the horizon where the dreams of a community united in health and well-being awaited. They knew that with every policy they crafted, every barrier they broke down, and every hand they held in solidarity, they were not just building infrastructure but forging a future where access to healthcare was a right, not a privilege.

Healthcare Financing and Insurance

"Healing Hearts, Securing Futures"

Under the canopy of the ancient baobab tree, the villagers of Kasama gathered once again, their spirits uplifted with anticipation. Today, Chilufya and his team continued their exploration of healthcare policy and public health, delving into the crucial realm of healthcare financing and insurance—a pathway toward ensuring that no one's health was compromised due to financial constraints. With the "Building Better

Communities" handbook illuminating their way, they embarked on a journey to secure the futures of their community through accessible and affordable healthcare.

Chilufya's voice carried on the breeze as he addressed the assembly, emphasizing the fundamental right of every individual to access quality healthcare without the burden of financial hardship. He spoke of the families torn apart by the inability to afford medical care, the children denied treatment due to poverty, and the imperative to build a healthcare system that provided financial security alongside medical assistance.

To delve deeper into the realm of healthcare financing and insurance, Chilufya and his team ventured across Zambia, their hearts heavy with the stories of those who had suffered due to inadequate financial protection. Their first destination was the bustling city of Kitwe, where the streets buzzed with the hustle and bustle of urban life.

In Kitwe, they were greeted by Mr. Banda, a healthcare economist with a vision as expansive as the African plains. He led them through the corridors of the hospital, where patients grappled with the dual burden of illness and financial strain.

As they navigated the labyrinth of healthcare financing, Chilufya and his team gained a deeper understanding of the inequities that plagued their healthcare system. Mr. Banda spoke of the importance of universal healthcare coverage, of pooling resources to ensure that everyone had access to essential services, and of the need for policy reforms that prioritized financial protection alongside medical care.

Next, the team journeyed to the rural heartlands of Southern Province, where the rhythms of life flowed with the gentle cadence of the land. There, they met with Mrs. Mwamba, a community health worker with a heart as warm as the African sun.

Mrs. Mwamba shared tales of the families she served, of the struggles they faced to afford even the most basic healthcare services. She spoke of the importance of community-based insurance schemes, of pooling resources to spread the financial risk, and of the need for policy reforms that empowered communities to take control of their healthcare futures.

Inspired by what they had witnessed, Chilufya and his team returned to Kasama, their hearts heavy with the weight of responsibility. They convened a meeting under the baobab tree, inviting healthcare workers, policymakers, and community leaders to join them on their journey to ensure financial security for all.

Chilufya shared the stories of Kitwe and Southern Province, of the hospitals and the rural villages, illustrating the urgent need for healthcare financing reforms that would provide a safety net for the most vulnerable members of their community. He spoke of the importance of healthcare policy and public health in ensuring that no one was left behind due to financial constraints.

One of the local healthcare workers, Nurse Mulenga, spoke of the transformative power of financial protection and the need to prioritize the most vulnerable in their community. "By investing in healthcare financing and insurance, we can ensure that every member of our community has the financial security they need to access essential services," she declared, her voice filled with determination.

The villagers nodded in agreement, their eyes alight with the fire of solidarity. They spoke of building a healthcare system that provided not only medical care but also financial security, of pooling resources to spread the risk, and of ensuring that no one had to choose between their health and their livelihood.

The local councilors pledged their support, promising to invest in healthcare financing reforms and community-based insurance schemes that would lay the foundation for a more equitable, more resilient future for Kasama. They agreed to work hand in hand with the community, ensuring that every step they took toward healthcare financing and insurance was a step toward healing and hope for all.

As the sun dipped below the horizon, casting a golden glow over the village, Chilufya stood before the gathered multitude. "We have learned that by embracing healthcare financing and insurance, we can ensure that every member of our community has the financial security they need to access essential services," he declared, his voice echoing through the gathering. "Let us embark on this journey together, with compassion and determination, knowing that every step we take toward financial protection is a step toward a healthier, more secure future."

With unity in their hearts and purpose in their steps, Chilufya and his team set forth, their eyes fixed on the horizon where the dreams of a community united in health and financial security awaited. They knew that with every policy they crafted, every reform they championed, and every hand they held in solidarity, they were not just building infrastructure but securing the futures of their community, one healed heart at a time.

Healthcare Promotion and Disease Prevention

"Guardians of Wellness, Architects of Prevention"

Underneath the sprawling branches of the ancient baobab tree, the villagers of Kasama convened once more, their faces alight with anticipation. Today, Chilufya and his team delved deeper into the realm of healthcare policy and public health, focusing on the pivotal aspect of healthcare promotion and disease prevention—a beacon guiding their community toward a future of wellness and vitality. With the "Building Better Communities" handbook illuminating their path, they embarked on a journey to empower their community with the knowledge and tools to safeguard their health.

Chilufya's voice resonated with passion as he addressed the gathering, emphasizing the importance of proactive measures in maintaining individual and community well-being. He spoke of the power of prevention, of the simple yet profound actions that could stave off illness and promote longevity, and of the imperative to embed healthcare promotion and disease prevention at the core of their healthcare system.

To delve deeper into the realm of healthcare promotion and disease prevention, Chilufya and his team ventured across the landscape of Zambia, their hearts buoyed by the promise of a healthier future. Their first destination was the bustling town of Ndola, where health educators and community activists worked tirelessly to promote healthy behaviors.

In Ndola, they were greeted by Ms. Chanda, a passionate health educator with a spirit as vibrant as the African sunrise. She led them through the streets, where posters and banners proclaimed the importance of vaccination, hand hygiene, and nutrition in preventing disease.

As they immersed themselves in the colorful tapestry of

health promotion initiatives, Chilufya and his team gained a deeper understanding of the transformative impact of community engagement. Ms. Chanda spoke of the importance of education in empowering individuals to take control of their health, of the need for targeted interventions to address specific health challenges, and of the role of policy in fostering a culture of prevention.

Next, the team journeyed to the verdant hills of Eastern Province, where the rhythms of life danced to the beat of the drum. There, they met with Mr. Phiri, a traditional healer with a reverence for the healing power of nature.

Mr. Phiri shared tales of ancient remedies passed down through generations, of herbs and plants that held the keys to wellness and vitality. He spoke of the importance of integrating traditional medicine into modern healthcare systems, of honoring indigenous knowledge, and of the need for policy reforms that recognized the holistic nature of health.

Inspired by what they had witnessed, Chilufya and his team returned to Kasama, their hearts ablaze with the fire of possibility. They convened a meeting under the baobab tree, inviting health workers, educators, and community leaders to join them on their journey to promote health and prevent disease.

Chilufya shared the stories of Ndola and Eastern Province, of the bustling town and the remote hills, illustrating the power of prevention in safeguarding individual and community well-being. He spoke of the importance of healthcare policy and public health in fostering a culture of prevention, of empowering individuals to make healthy choices, and of harnessing the wisdom of traditional medicine to complement modern healthcare systems.

One of the local educators, Mr. Mumba, spoke of the transformative potential of health promotion and disease prevention and the need to prioritize wellness in their community. "By investing in healthcare promotion and disease prevention, we can empower individuals to take control of their health and build a future of vitality and resilience," he declared, his voice filled with conviction.

The villagers nodded in agreement, their eyes alight with the fire of empowerment. They spoke of spreading knowledge, of fostering healthy habits, and of nurturing a culture of prevention that would ripple through their community, touching every life with the promise of wellness.

The local councilors pledged their support, promising to invest in health promotion initiatives and disease prevention programs that would lay the foundation for a healthier, more resilient future for Kasama. They agreed to work hand in hand with the community, ensuring that every step they took toward healthcare promotion and disease prevention was a step toward empowerment and vitality for all.

As the sun dipped below the horizon, casting a golden glow over the village, Chilufya stood before the gathered multitude. "We have learned that by embracing healthcare promotion and disease prevention, we can empower individuals to take control of their health and build a future of vitality and resilience," he declared, his voice echoing through the gathering. "Let us embark on this journey together, with determination and dedication, knowing that every step we take toward prevention is a step toward a healthier, more vibrant future."

With unity in their hearts and purpose in their steps,

Chilufya and his team set forth, their eyes fixed on the horizon where the dreams of a community united in wellness awaited. They knew that with every policy they crafted, every initiative they launched, and every hand they held in solidarity, they were not just building infrastructure but laying the groundwork for a future where health was not just the absence of illness but the presence of vitality and joy.

Mental Health Policy and Support Systems

"Harmony of Minds, Sanctuary of Souls"

Beneath the timeless embrace of the ancient baobab tree, the villagers of Kasama gathered once more, their spirits intertwined with hope and empathy. Today, Chilufya and his team delved deeper into the realm of healthcare policy and public health, focusing on the often-overlooked domain of mental health policy and support systems—a sanctuary for the mind and the soul. With the "Building Better Communities" handbook illuminating their path, they embarked on a journey to nurture mental well-being and foster resilience within their community.

Chilufya's voice carried on the gentle breeze as he addressed the assembly, emphasizing the intrinsic connection between mental and physical health. He spoke of the silent struggles that burdened the soul, the stigma that shrouded mental illness, and the imperative to build a healthcare system that offered solace and support to those in need.

To explore the realm of mental health policy and support systems, Chilufya and his team ventured across Zambia, their hearts heavy with the stories of those who had grappled with the shadows of the mind. Their first destination was the bustling city of Livingstone, where mental health professionals and advocates labored tirelessly to break the chains of silence and stigma.

In Livingstone, they were greeted by Dr. Mulenga, a compassionate psychiatrist with a heart as vast as the Zambezi River. She led them through the corridors of the psychiatric hospital, where patients sought refuge from the storms within.

As they immersed themselves in the delicate dance of healing, Chilufya and his team gained a deeper understanding of the complexities that surrounded mental health care. Dr. Mulenga spoke of the importance of destigmatizing mental illness, of providing accessible and culturally sensitive services, and of the need for policy reforms that prioritized mental well-being alongside physical health.

Next, the team journeyed to the tranquil hills of Northern Province, where the whispers of the wind carried the echoes of ancient wisdom. There, they met with Elder Mwape, a revered healer with a reverence for the interconnectedness of mind, body, and spirit.

Elder Mwape shared tales of the healing rituals that had sustained his people for generations, of the bond between community and individual, and of the need to reclaim mental health as a cornerstone of holistic well-being. He spoke of the importance of integrating traditional healing practices into modern healthcare systems, of honoring diverse perspectives, and of the need for policy reforms that recognized the richness of human experience.

Inspired by what they had witnessed, Chilufya and his team returned to Kasama, their hearts brimming with compassion. They convened a meeting under the baobab tree, inviting mental health professionals, community leaders, and advocates to join them on their journey to nurture mental well-being.

Chilufya shared the stories of Livingstone and Northern Province, of the bustling city and the tranquil hills, illustrating the urgent need for mental health policy reforms that would dismantle stigma and provide support to those in need. He spoke of the importance of healthcare policy and public health in fostering a culture of compassion, of empowering individuals to seek help without fear or shame, and of the role of community in healing and resilience.

One of the local advocates, Ms. Ngosa, spoke of the transformative power of mental health support systems and the need to prioritize well-being in their community. "By investing in mental health policy reforms and support systems, we can create a sanctuary for the mind and the soul," she declared, her voice resolute with determination.

The villagers nodded in agreement, their eyes alight with the fire of empathy. They spoke of breaking the chains of stigma, of providing sanctuary for the wounded soul, and of nurturing resilience in the face of adversity.

The local councilors pledged their support, promising to invest in mental health policy reforms and community-based support systems that would lay the foundation for a more compassionate, more resilient future for Kasama. They agreed to work hand in hand with the community, ensuring that every step they took toward mental well-being was a step toward healing and hope for all.

As the sun dipped below the horizon, casting a golden glow over the village, Chilufya stood before the gathered multitude. "We have learned that by embracing mental health policy and support systems, we can create a sanctuary for the mind and the soul," he declared, his voice echoing through the gathering. "Let us embark on this journey together, with empathy and determination, knowing that every step we take toward mental well-being is a step toward a healthier, more resilient future."

With unity in their hearts and purpose in their steps, Chilufya and his team set forth, their eyes fixed on the horizon where the dreams of a community united in compassion and resilience awaited. They knew that with every policy they crafted, every stigma they shattered, and every hand they held in solidarity, they were not just building infrastructure but nurturing the very essence of humanity—the harmony of minds, the sanctuary of souls.

Healthcare Quality and Patient Safety

"Guardians of Care, Sentinels of Safety"

Beneath the ancient baobab tree, its sprawling branches casting dappled shadows on the gathered villagers, Chilufya and his team reconvened once more. Today, they delved further into the realm of healthcare policy and public health, focusing on the critical aspect of healthcare quality and patient safety—a cornerstone of trust and assurance in the healing process. With the "Building Better Communities" handbook guiding their endeavors, they embarked on a journey to ensure that every interaction with the healthcare system was characterized by excellence and security.

Chilufya's voice rang out with conviction as he addressed the assembly, emphasizing the sacred duty of healthcare providers to deliver care that was not only effective but also safe and compassionate. He spoke of the trust that patients placed in their healers, the responsibility that lay heavy upon the shoulders of caregivers, and the imperative to build a healthcare system that upheld the highest standards of quality and safety.

To explore the realm of healthcare quality and patient safety, Chilufya and his team embarked on a journey across Zambia, their hearts heavy with the stories of those who had suffered due to lapses in care. Their first destination was the bustling town of Kabwe, where the halls of the local hospital echoed with the hustle and bustle of medical activity.

In Kabwe, they were greeted by Nurse Chanda, a dedicated healthcare professional with a commitment to excellence that shone like a beacon in the darkness. She led them through the corridors of the hospital, where patients lay in beds, their eyes reflecting a mix of hope and apprehension.

As they navigated the maze of medical procedures and protocols, Chilufya and his team gained a deeper understanding of the complexities that surrounded healthcare delivery. Nurse Chanda spoke of the importance of continuous training and education for healthcare providers, of the need for robust systems to monitor and report adverse events, and of the role of policy in fostering a culture of safety and accountability.

Next, the team journeyed to the remote village of Chinsali, nestled in the verdant hills of Northern Province, where the rhythms of life flowed with the gentle cadence of tradition. There, they met with Elder Mulenga, a respected community leader with a wisdom that transcended generations.

Elder Mulenga shared tales of healers and herbalists who had tended to the sick since time immemorial, of the trust that had been built through centuries of care, and of the need to integrate traditional wisdom with modern practices. He spoke of the importance of patient-centered care, of listening to the voices of those in need, and of the role of policy in ensuring that every patient was treated with dignity and respect.

Inspired by what they had witnessed, Chilufya and his team returned to Kasama, their hearts filled with determination. They convened a meeting under the baobab tree, inviting healthcare providers, policymakers, and community leaders to join them on their journey to ensure healthcare quality and patient safety.

Chilufya shared the stories of Kabwe and Chinsali, of the bustling town and the remote village, illustrating the urgent need for healthcare policy reforms that would prioritize excellence and security in care delivery. He spoke of the importance of healthcare policy and public health in fostering a culture of safety and accountability, of empowering patients to be partners in their own care, and of the role of community in upholding the highest standards of quality.

One of the local nurses, Ms. Bwalya, spoke of the transformative power of healthcare quality and patient safety and the need to prioritize the well-being of every individual in their community. "By investing in healthcare policy reforms and patient safety initiatives, we can ensure that every interaction with the healthcare system is characterized by excellence and security," she declared, her voice resolute with determination.

The villagers nodded in agreement, their eyes alight with the fire of advocacy. They spoke of guardianship and stewardship, of vigilance and compassion, and of nurturing a culture of safety that would envelop every member of their community in a cocoon of care.

The local councilors pledged their support, promising to

invest in healthcare quality initiatives and patient safety measures that would lay the foundation for a more trustworthy, more resilient future for Kasama. They agreed to work hand in hand with the community, ensuring that every step they took toward healthcare quality and patient safety was a step toward excellence and security for all.

As the sun dipped below the horizon, casting a golden glow over the village, Chilufya stood before the gathered multitude. "We have learned that by embracing healthcare quality and patient safety, we can ensure that every interaction with the healthcare system is characterized by excellence and security," he declared, his voice echoing through the gathering. "Let us embark on this journey together, with diligence and compassion, knowing that every step we take toward quality and safety is a step toward a healthier, more trustworthy future."

With unity in their hearts and purpose in their steps, Chilufya and his team set forth, their eyes fixed on the horizon where the dreams of a community united in excellence and security awaited. They knew that with every policy they crafted, every protocol they implemented, and every hand they held in solidarity, they were not just building infrastructure but safeguarding the very essence of care—the guardians of healing, the sentinels of safety.

Global Health Challenges and Cooperation

"Bridging Borders, Healing Humanity"

Under the majestic canopy of the ancient baobab tree, the villagers of Kasama gathered once again, their faces radiant with curiosity and compassion. Today, Chilufya and his team embarked on a journey beyond their borders, exploring the global landscape of healthcare policy and public health. With the "Building Better Communities" handbook as their guide, they sought to understand the interconnectedness of health challenges across the world and the power of collaboration in overcoming them.

Chilufya's voice resonated with sincerity as he addressed the assembly, emphasizing the shared responsibility of humanity to address health challenges that transcended borders. He spoke of the infectious diseases that knew no boundaries, the disparities in access to care that spanned continents, and the imperative to build a healthcare system that embraced solidarity and cooperation on a global scale.

To explore the realm of global health challenges and co-operation, Chilufya and his team embarked on a virtual journey across continents, their hearts heavy with the weight of suffering and hope. They connected with healthcare professionals and policymakers from around the world, seeking to understand the diverse perspectives and experiences that shaped the global health landscape.

Their first destination was the bustling city of Geneva, where the headquarters of the World Health Organization stood as a beacon of hope in the fight against disease and despair. There, they met with Dr. Amadi, a passionate advocate for health equity and justice.

Dr. Amadi shared tales of the global efforts to combat infectious diseases such as malaria, tuberculosis, and HIV/AIDS, of the partnerships forged between nations to ensure access to life-saving treatments and vaccines, and of the challenges that remained in achieving health for all. He spoke of the importance of solidarity and cooperation in addressing global health challenges, of pooling resources and expertise to tackle shared threats, and of the need for policy reforms that prioritized equity and justice.

Next, the team journeyed to the remote villages of the Amazon rainforest, where the rhythms of life danced to the beat of nature's symphony. There, they met with Shaman Alvarez, a healer whose wisdom was rooted in ancient traditions.

Shaman Alvarez shared tales of the healing plants that flourished in the heart of the jungle, of the balance between humanity and nature that sustained his people for generations, and of the threats posed by deforestation and environmental degradation. He spoke of the interconnectedness of health and the environment, of the need to safeguard the planet for future generations, and of the role of policy in promoting sustainability and resilience.

Inspired by what they had learned, Chilufya and his team returned to Kasama, their hearts filled with a renewed sense of purpose. They convened a meeting under the baobab tree, inviting community members, healthcare providers, and policymakers to join them on their journey to embrace global health challenges and cooperation.

Chilufya shared the stories of Geneva and the Amazon rainforest, of the bustling city and the remote villages, illustrating the urgent need for global solidarity in addressing health challenges. He spoke of the importance of healthcare policy and public health in fostering cooperation and collaboration, of working together as a global community to build a future where health was a right, not a privilege.

One of the local nurses, Ms. Banda, spoke of the transformative power of global health cooperation and the need to prioritize solidarity in their community. "By embracing global health challenges and cooperation, we can build a future where every member of our community has access to the care they need to thrive," she declared, her voice filled with conviction.

The villagers nodded in agreement, their eyes alight with the fire of unity. They spoke of bridging borders and breaking down barriers, of recognizing the humanity in every individual, and of nurturing a culture of cooperation that would transcend geography and ideology.

The local councilors pledged their support, promising to invest in policies and programs that promoted global health cooperation and solidarity. They agreed to work hand in hand with the community, ensuring that every step they took toward global health was a step toward healing and hope for all.

As the sun dipped below the horizon, casting a golden glow over the village, Chilufya stood before the gathered multitude. "We have learned that by embracing global health challenges and cooperation, we can build a future where health is a universal right and humanity is united in healing and hope," he declared, his voice echoing through the gathering. "Let us embark on this journey together, with compassion and solidarity, knowing that every step we take toward global health is a step toward a healthier, more equitable future for all."

With unity in their hearts and purpose in their steps,

Chilufya and his team set forth, their eyes fixed on the horizon where the dreams of a community united in compassion and cooperation awaited. They knew that with every policy they crafted, every partnership they forged, and every hand they held in solidarity, they were not just building infrastructure but weaving a tapestry of healing and humanity that spanned the globe.

9

Chapter 9: Education Policy and Lifelong Learning

Early Childhood Education Initiatives

"Seeds of Knowledge, Roots of Opportunity"

Beneath the sprawling branches of the ancient baobab tree, the villagers of Kasama gathered once more, their eyes brimming with anticipation and aspiration. Today, Chilufya and his team embarked on a journey to explore the transformative power of education policy and lifelong learning, with a special focus on early childhood education initiatives—the seeds from which the forests of knowledge and opportunity would grow. With the "Building Better Communities" handbook as their compass, they set out to sow the seeds of wisdom and nurture the minds of tomorrow.

Chilufya's voice resonated with warmth as he addressed the gathering, emphasizing the pivotal role of early childhood education in laying the foundation for a lifetime of learning and growth. He spoke of the boundless potential that lay within each child, the importance of nurturing curiosity and creativity from a young age, and the imperative to build an education system that embraced the needs of every learner.

To explore the realm of early childhood education initiatives, Chilufya and his team ventured across Kasama, their hearts filled with the laughter and innocence of childhood. Their first destination was the bustling town of Solwezi, where the corridors of the local preschool echoed with the sounds of exploration and discovery.

In Solwezi, they were greeted by Teacher Mwansa, a dedicated educator with a heart as big as the African sky. She led them through the colorful classrooms, where children with bright eyes and eager minds embarked on a journey of learning and play.

As they observed the wonders of early childhood education in action, Chilufya and his team gained a deeper understanding of its transformative impact. Teacher Mwansa spoke of the importance of play-based learning in fostering social and emotional development, of the need for inclusive practices that embraced diversity and equity, and of the role of policy in ensuring access to quality early childhood education for all.

Next, the team journeyed to the rural villages of North-Western Province, where the rhythms of life echoed the timeless wisdom of the land. There, they met with Grandmother Kasonde, a respected elder with a wealth of knowledge passed down through generations.

Grandmother Kasonde shared tales of the traditional wisdom that had guided her people for centuries, of the importance of storytelling and song in nurturing young minds, and of the need to integrate indigenous knowledge into modern education systems. She spoke of the interconnectedness of community and learning, of the role of elders as guardians of wisdom, and of the imperative to build bridges between past and present, tradition and innovation.

Inspired by what they had witnessed, Chilufya and his team returned to Kasama, their hearts brimming with hope. They convened a meeting under the baobab tree, inviting educators, parents, and community leaders to join them on their journey to embrace early childhood education initiatives.

Chilufya shared the stories of Solwezi and North-Western Province, of the bustling town and the rural villages, illustrating the transformative power of early childhood education in shaping the future. He spoke of the importance of education policy and lifelong learning in nurturing the seeds of knowledge, of investing in the early years as a pathway to prosperity and equity, and of the role of community in fostering a culture of learning and growth.

One of the local parents, Mrs. Simukonda, spoke of the transformative impact of early childhood education initiatives and the need to prioritize investment in the youngest members of their community. "By embracing early childhood education initiatives, we can unlock the potential of every child and build a future where opportunity knows no bounds," she declared, her voice filled with conviction.

The villagers nodded in agreement, their eyes alight with the fire of possibility. They spoke of nurturing potential and fostering curiosity, of creating a world where every child could thrive and succeed, and of the role of education in building a brighter tomorrow.

The local councilors pledged their support, promising to

invest in early childhood education initiatives and policies that would lay the foundation for a more prosperous, more equitable future for Kasama. They agreed to work hand in hand with the community, ensuring that every step they took toward education and lifelong learning was a step toward empowerment and opportunity for all.

As the sun dipped below the horizon, casting a golden glow over the village, Chilufya stood before the gathered multitude. "We have learned that by embracing early childhood education initiatives, we can sow the seeds of knowledge and opportunity for generations to come," he declared, his voice echoing through the gathering. "Let us embark on this journey together, with compassion and dedication, knowing that every child we nurture is a beacon of hope for the future."

With unity in their hearts and purpose in their steps, Chilufya and his team set forth, their eyes fixed on the horizon where the dreams of a community united in learning and growth awaited. They knew that with every policy they crafted, every lesson they taught, and every hand they held in solidarity, they were not just building infrastructure but nurturing the minds and hearts of tomorrow—the seeds of knowledge, the roots of opportunity.

K-12 Education Reforms

"Forging Futures, Shaping Minds"

Under the expansive canopy of the ancient baobab tree, the villagers of Kasama congregated once more, their faces alight with curiosity and determination. Today, Chilufya and his team delved deeper into the realm of education policy and lifelong learning, focusing on the transformative potential of K-12 education reforms—the scaffolding upon which dreams are built and futures forged. With the "Building Better Communities" handbook as their guiding light, they embarked on a journey to reimagine the landscape of education and empower every child to reach for the stars.

Chilufya's voice carried on the gentle breeze as he addressed the assembly, emphasizing the profound impact of K-12 education reforms in shaping the trajectory of young lives. He spoke of the need for a curriculum that fostered critical thinking and creativity, of the imperative to provide teachers with the support and resources they needed to succeed, and of the role of policy in ensuring equity and excellence in education for all.

To explore the realm of K-12 education reforms, Chilufya and his team ventured across Kasama, their hearts filled with the hopes and aspirations of the next generation. Their first destination was the bustling city of Lusaka, where the halls of the Ministry of Education buzzed with activity and innovation.

In Lusaka, they were greeted by Minister Kabwe, a visionary leader with a passion for educational equity and excellence. She led them through the corridors of power, where policies and programs were crafted to shape the future of education in Zambia.

As they immersed themselves in the complexities of education reform, Chilufya and his team gained a deeper understanding of the challenges and opportunities that lay ahead. Minister Kabwe spoke of the importance of inclusive and learner-centered approaches to education, of the need to invest in teacher training and professional development, and of the role of policy in driving systemic change.

Next, the team journeyed to the rural schools of Western Province, where the rhythms of life echoed the timeless wisdom of the land. There, they met with Head Teacher Mwamba, a dedicated educator with a heart as big as the African sky.

Head Teacher Mwamba shared tales of the challenges faced by schools in remote areas, of the resilience and resourcefulness of teachers and students alike, and of the need to tailor education reforms to meet the unique needs of every community. He spoke of the importance of empowering schools to innovate and adapt, of the role of technology in expanding access to quality education, and of the imperative to build bridges between urban and rural, tradition and innovation.

Inspired by what they had witnessed, Chilufya and his team returned to Kasama, their hearts brimming with possibility. They convened a meeting under the baobab tree, inviting educators, parents, and community leaders to join them on their journey to embrace K-12 education reforms.

Chilufya shared the stories of Lusaka and Western Province, of the bustling city and the rural schools, illustrating the urgent need for education policy reforms that would empower every child to reach their full potential. He spoke of the importance of lifelong learning and adaptability in a rapidly changing world, of investing in the skills and knowledge that would prepare students for the challenges of tomorrow, and of the role of community in shaping the future of education.

One of the local teachers, Mr. Phiri, spoke of the transformative power of K-12 education reforms and the need to prioritize investment in the youngest members of their community. "By embracing education policy reforms, we can unlock the potential of every child and build a future where opportunity knows no bounds," he declared, his voice filled with conviction.

The villagers nodded in agreement, their eyes alight with the fire of possibility. They spoke of nurturing talent and fostering ambition, of creating a world where every child could thrive and succeed, and of the role of education in building a brighter tomorrow.

The local councilors pledged their support, promising to invest in education policy reforms and programs that would lay the foundation for a more prosperous, more equitable future for Kasama. They agreed to work hand in hand with the community, ensuring that every step they took toward education and lifelong learning was a step toward empowerment and opportunity for all.

As the sun dipped below the horizon, casting a golden glow over the village, Chilufya stood before the gathered multitude. "We have learned that by embracing K-12 education reforms, we can shape the minds and futures of generations to come," he declared, his voice echoing through the gathering. "Let us embark on this journey together, with determination and dedication, knowing that every child we educate is a beacon of hope for the future."

With unity in their hearts and purpose in their steps, Chilufya and his team set forth, their eyes fixed on the horizon where the dreams of a community united in learning and growth awaited. They knew that with every policy they crafted, every lesson they taught, and every hand they held in solidarity, they were not just building infrastructure but shaping the destiny of a nation—the seeds of knowledge, the roots of opportunity.

Higher Education Policies and Accessibility

"Horizons Unbounded, Minds Unleashed"

Under the expansive canopy of the ancient baobab tree, the villagers of Kasama gathered once again, their faces aglow with anticipation and possibility. Today, Chilufya and his team embarked on a journey to explore the transformative power of higher education policies and accessibility—the gateways to boundless horizons and unleashed potential. With the "Building Better Communities" handbook as their compass, they set out to pave the way for every aspiring mind to reach for the stars.

Chilufya's voice resonated with fervor as he addressed the assembly, emphasizing the profound impact of higher education in shaping the trajectory of individual lives and the collective future. He spoke of the imperative to tear down barriers to access, to ensure that every young person had the opportunity to pursue their dreams and contribute to the advancement of society.

To explore the realm of higher education policies and accessibility, Chilufya and his team journeyed across Kasama, their hearts filled with the dreams and aspirations of the youth. Their first destination was the bustling city of Ndola, where the halls of the university thrummed with the energy of knowledge seekers.

In Ndola, they were greeted by Professor Mwaba, a passionate educator with a vision for a more inclusive and equitable higher education system. She led them through the corridors of learning, where students from diverse backgrounds converged to expand their minds and broaden their horizons.

As they immersed themselves in the vibrancy of university life, Chilufya and his team gained a deeper understanding of the challenges and opportunities that lay ahead. Professor Mwaba spoke of the importance of affordability and financial aid in ensuring access to higher education, of the need for diverse and inclusive curricula that reflected the richness of human experience, and of the role of policy in driving systemic change.

Next, the team journeyed to the rural communities of Southern Province, where the rhythms of life echoed the timeless wisdom of the land. There, they met with Isaac, a bright young man whose dreams of higher education seemed out of reach.

Isaac shared tales of the obstacles he faced—financial hardship, lack of access to quality schools, and a sense of hopelessness that threatened to extinguish his aspirations. He spoke of the transformative power of education, of the dreams that burned within him despite the odds, and of the urgent need for policies that would level the playing field and unlock the doors of opportunity for all.

Inspired by Isaac's resilience, Chilufya and his team returned to Kasama, their hearts brimming with determination. They convened a meeting under the baobab tree, inviting educators, policymakers, and community leaders to join them on their journey to embrace higher education policies and accessibility.

Chilufya shared the stories of Ndola and Southern Province, of the bustling city and the rural communities, illustrating the urgent need for policies that would tear down barriers to access and empower every young person to reach their full potential. He spoke of the importance of lifelong learning and continuous skill development in a rapidly changing world, of investing in the talents and aspirations of the youth, and of the role of community in shaping the future of higher education.

One of the local students, Mary, spoke of the transformative power of higher education policies and the need to prioritize investment in the future of their community. "By embracing higher education policies and accessibility, we can unleash the potential of every young person and build a future where opportunity knows no bounds," she declared, her voice filled with conviction.

The villagers nodded in agreement, their eyes alight with the fire of possibility. They spoke of breaking down barriers and opening doors, of creating a world where every young person could pursue their dreams and make a difference, and of the role of education in building a brighter tomorrow.

The local councilors pledged their support, promising to invest in higher education policies and programs that would lay the foundation for a more prosperous, more equitable future for Kasama. They agreed to work hand in hand with the community, ensuring that every step they took toward education and accessibility was a step toward empowerment and opportunity for all.

As the sun dipped below the horizon, casting a golden glow over the village, Chilufya stood before the gathered multitude. "We have learned that by embracing higher education policies and accessibility, we can unlock the potential of every young person and build a future where opportunity knows no bounds," he declared, his voice echoing through the gathering. "Let us embark on this journey together, with determination and dedication, knowing that every mind we unleash is a beacon of hope for the future."

With unity in their hearts and purpose in their steps, Chilufya and his team set forth, their eyes fixed on the horizon where the dreams of a community united in learning and growth awaited. They knew that with every policy they crafted, every opportunity they opened, and every hand they held in solidarity, they were not just building infrastructure but shaping the destiny of a nation—the gateways to boundless horizons, the minds unleashed.

Vocational Training and Skills Development

"Crafting Futures, Forging Skills"

Beneath the shade of the majestic baobab tree, the villagers of Kasama gathered once more, their hearts brimming with anticipation and resolve. Today, Chilufya and his team embarked on a journey to explore the transformative power of vocational training and skills development—the crucibles where raw potential is honed into mastery and opportunity. With the "Building Better Communities" handbook as their compass, they set out to pave the way for every individual to unleash their talents and thrive in the world of work.

Chilufya's voice resonated with determination as he addressed the assembly, emphasizing the vital role of vocational training and skills development in equipping individuals with the tools they need to succeed in the workforce. He spoke of the imperative to nurture a culture of lifelong learning, to ensure that every member of the community had the opportunity to acquire the skills they needed to thrive in an ever-evolving economy.

To explore the realm of vocational training and skills development, Chilufya and his team ventured across Kasama, their hearts filled with the dreams and aspirations of those seeking to carve out their place in the world. Their first destination was the bustling town of Kitwe, where the clang of machinery and the hum of industry filled the air.

In Kitwe, they were greeted by Mr. Mulenga, a seasoned artisan with a passion for passing on his craft to the next generation. He led them through the workshops and training centers, where young apprentices honed their skills under the guidance of master craftsmen.

As they immersed themselves in the world of vocational training, Chilufya and his team gained a deeper understanding of the power of hands-on learning and practical experience. Mr. Mulenga spoke of the importance of apprenticeships in bridging the gap between education and employment, of the need for partnerships between industry and academia to ensure that training programs met the needs of the market, and of the role of policy in promoting innovation and entrepreneurship.

Next, the team journeyed to the rural communities of Eastern Province, where the rhythms of life echoed the timeless wisdom of the land. There, they met with Grace, a young woman with a passion for agriculture and a desire to build a better future for her family.

Grace shared tales of the challenges faced by rural youth—limited access to education and training opportunities, lack of infrastructure and resources, and a sense of isolation that threatened to stifle their dreams. She spoke of the transformative power of vocational training, of the skills she had acquired through hands-on experience and mentorship, and of the urgent need for policies that would expand access to training programs and support rural youth in pursuing their aspirations.

Inspired by Grace's resilience, Chilufya and his team returned to Kasama, their hearts brimming with determination. They convened a meeting under the baobab tree, inviting educators, policymakers, and community leaders to join them on their journey to embrace vocational training and skills development.

Chilufya shared the stories of Kitwe and Eastern Province, of the bustling town and the rural communities, illustrating the urgent need for policies that would unlock the potential of every individual and empower them to build a better future for themselves and their communities. He spoke of the importance of practical experience and mentorship in fostering talent and innovation, of investing in vocational training as a pathway to prosperity and self-sufficiency, and of the role of community in shaping the future of skills development.

One of the local artisans, Mr. Nyirenda, spoke of the transformative power of vocational training and the need to prioritize investment in the skills of their community members. "By embracing vocational training and skills development, we can unleash the potential of every individual and build a future where opportunity knows no bounds," he declared, his voice filled with conviction.

The villagers nodded in agreement, their eyes alight with the fire of possibility. They spoke of crafting futures and forging skills, of creating a world where every individual could thrive and contribute to the prosperity of their community, and of the role of education in building a brighter tomorrow.

The local councilors pledged their support, promising to invest in vocational training policies and programs that would lay the foundation for a more prosperous, more equitable future for Kasama. They agreed to work hand in hand with the community, ensuring that every step they took toward skills development was a step toward empowerment and opportunity for all.

As the sun dipped below the horizon, casting a golden glow over the village, Chilufya stood before the gathered multitude. "We have learned that by embracing vocational training and skills development, we can unlock the potential of every individual and build a future where opportunity knows no bounds," he declared, his voice echoing through the gathering. "Let us embark on this journey together, with determination and dedication, knowing that every skill we forge is a step toward a brighter, more prosperous future."

With unity in their hearts and purpose in their steps, Chilufya and his team set forth, their eyes fixed on the horizon where the dreams of a community united in learning and growth awaited. They knew that with every policy they crafted, every opportunity they opened, and every hand they held in solidarity, they were not just building infrastructure but shaping the destiny of a nation—the crafts of the trade, the futures forged.

Lifelong Learning Opportunities

"Eternal Springs of Knowledge"

Under the serene canopy of the ancient baobab tree, the villagers of Kasama gathered once more, their spirits buoyed by the promise of lifelong learning and endless possibilities. Today, Chilufya and his team embarked on a journey to explore the transformative power of lifelong learning opportunities—the perennial springs from which wisdom flows, nourishing minds and hearts for generations to come. With the "Building Better Communities" handbook as their guide, they set out to cultivate a culture of curiosity and growth that would enrich the fabric of their community.

Chilufya's voice carried on the gentle breeze as he addressed the assembly, emphasizing the timeless importance of lifelong learning in a rapidly changing world. He spoke of the imperative to embrace curiosity and adaptability, to cultivate a thirst for knowledge that transcended age and circumstance, and to ensure that every member of the community had the opportunity to pursue learning throughout their lives.

To explore the realm of lifelong learning opportunities, Chilufya and his team ventured across Kasama, their hearts filled with the dreams and aspirations of those seeking to expand their horizons. Their first destination was the bustling city of Livingstone, where the halls of the community center buzzed with activity and excitement.

In Livingstone, they were greeted by Mrs. Banda, a lifelong learner with a passion for exploring new horizons and pushing the boundaries of her own understanding. She led them through the corridors of the center, where people of all ages and backgrounds came together to engage in a diverse array of educational programs and activities.

As they immersed themselves in the world of lifelong learning, Chilufya and his team gained a deeper understanding of its transformative power. Mrs. Banda spoke of the importance of creating inclusive and accessible learning environments, of the need to tailor programs to meet the diverse needs and interests of the community, and of the role of policy in promoting a culture of lifelong learning.

Next, the team journeyed to the rural villages of Northern Province, where the rhythms of life echoed the timeless wisdom of the land. There, they met with Mr. Tembo, an elder with a thirst for knowledge that burned as brightly as the African sun.

Mr. Tembo shared tales of the rich oral traditions that had sustained his community for generations, of the wisdom passed down through stories and songs that spoke to the essence of what it means to be human. He spoke of the importance of preserving and celebrating indigenous knowledge, of the role of elders as custodians of wisdom, and of the imperative to create spaces where people of all ages could come together to learn and grow.

Inspired by Mr. Tembo's wisdom, Chilufya and his team returned to Kasama, their hearts brimming with possibility. They convened a meeting under the baobab tree, inviting educators, policymakers, and community leaders to join them on their journey to embrace lifelong learning opportunities.

Chilufya shared the stories of Livingstone and Northern Province, of the bustling city and the rural villages, illustrating the transformative power of lifelong learning in enriching the lives of individuals and communities alike. He spoke of the importance of fostering a culture of curiosity and growth, of investing in programs and initiatives that would empower people of all ages to pursue their passions and fulfill their potential, and of the role of community in shaping the future of lifelong learning.

One of the local students, Samuel, spoke of the transformative impact of lifelong learning opportunities and the need to prioritize investment in education and personal development. "By embracing lifelong learning opportunities, we can unlock the potential of every individual and build a future where knowledge knows no bounds," he declared, his voice filled with conviction.

The villagers nodded in agreement, their eyes alight with the fire of possibility. They spoke of nurturing minds and hearts, of creating a world where learning was a lifelong journey of discovery and growth, and of the role of education in building a brighter tomorrow.

The local councilors pledged their support, promising to invest in lifelong learning policies and programs that would lay the foundation for a more prosperous, more equitable future for Kasama. They agreed to work hand in hand with the community, ensuring that every step they took toward lifelong learning was a step toward empowerment and opportunity for all.

As the sun dipped below the horizon, casting a golden glow over the village, Chilufya stood before the gathered multitude. "We have learned that by embracing lifelong learning opportunities, we can unlock the potential of every individual and build a future where wisdom flows like a river, nourishing minds and hearts for generations to come," he declared, his voice echoing through the gathering. "Let us embark on this journey together, with open minds and eager hearts, knowing that every step we take toward learning is a step toward a brighter, more enlightened future."

With unity in their hearts and purpose in their steps, Chilufya and his team set forth, their eyes fixed on the horizon where the eternal springs of knowledge awaited. They knew that with every policy they crafted, every opportunity they opened, and every hand they held in solidarity, they were not just building infrastructure but nurturing the seeds of wisdom—the lifelong learners, the eternal springs of knowledge.

Education Technology and Innovation

"Innovate to Educate: Pioneering Paths of Progress"

Beneath the sprawling branches of the ancient baobab tree, the villagers of Kasama convened once more, their spirits alight with the promise of education technology and innovation—the beacons guiding their journey into the future. Today, Chilufya and his team embarked on a quest to explore the transformative power of technological advancement in education—the catalysts igniting minds and illuminating pathways to progress. With the "Building Better Communities" handbook as their compass, they set forth to embrace innovation as the cornerstone of a brighter tomorrow.

Chilufya's voice resonated with vigor as he addressed the assembly, underscoring the pivotal role of education technology and innovation in shaping the educational landscape of the future. He spoke of the imperative to harness the power of technology to democratize access to knowledge, to foster creativity and critical thinking, and to empower learners of all ages to thrive in the digital age.

To explore the realm of education technology and innovation, Chilufya and his team embarked on a journey across Kasama, their hearts brimming with the possibilities of progress. Their first destination was the bustling city of Lusaka, where the pulse of innovation reverberated through the corridors of the technology hub.

In Lusaka, they were greeted by Dr. Musonda, a visionary technologist with a passion for leveraging technology to revolutionize education. She led them through the labs and incubators, where entrepreneurs and educators collaborated to develop cutting-edge solutions to the challenges facing learners in the 21st century.

As they immersed themselves in the world of education technology, Chilufya and his team gained a deeper understanding of its transformative potential. Dr. Musonda spoke of the importance of digital literacy and fluency in preparing learners for the future workforce, of the need to harness emerging technologies such as artificial intelligence and virtual reality to enhance teaching and learning experiences, and of the role of policy in fostering an ecosystem of innovation and entrepreneurship.

Next, the team journeyed to the rural communities of Western Province, where the rhythms of life echoed the timeless wisdom of the land. There, they met with Mr. Kamanga, a teacher with a passion for bringing the benefits of technology to underserved communities.

Mr. Kamanga shared tales of the challenges faced by rural schools—limited access to resources and connectivity, outdated infrastructure, and a lack of training opportunities for teachers. He spoke of the transformative power of education technology, of the ways in which digital tools could bridge the gap between urban and rural, rich and poor, and unlock new opportunities for learning and growth.

Inspired by Mr. Kamanga's dedication, Chilufya and his team returned to Kasama, their hearts brimming with determination. They convened a meeting under the baobab tree, inviting educators, policymakers, and community leaders to join them on their journey to embrace education technology and innovation.

Chilufya shared the stories of Lusaka and Western Province, of the bustling city and the rural communities, illustrating the urgent need for policies that would harness the power of technology to democratize access to education and empower learners of all ages. He spoke of the importance of investing in digital infrastructure and connectivity, of providing training and support for teachers to integrate technology into their classrooms, and of the role of community in shaping the future of education.

One of the local students, Esther, spoke of the transformative impact of education technology and the need to prioritize investment in digital innovation. "By embracing education technology and innovation, we can unlock the potential of every learner and build a future where knowledge knows no bounds," she declared, her voice filled with conviction.

The villagers nodded in agreement, their eyes alight with the fire of possibility. They spoke of pioneering paths of progress, of embracing innovation as the key to unlocking the doors of opportunity for future generations, and of the role of education technology in shaping a brighter tomorrow.

The local councilors pledged their support, promising to invest in education technology policies and programs that would lay the foundation for a more prosperous, more equitable future for Kasama. They agreed to work hand in hand with the community, ensuring that every step they took toward innovation was a step toward empowerment and opportunity for all.

As the sun dipped below the horizon, casting a golden glow over the village, Chilufya stood before the gathered multitude. "We have learned that by embracing education technology and innovation, we can unlock the potential of every learner and build a future where knowledge knows no bounds," he declared, his voice echoing through the gathering. "Let us embark on this journey together, with open minds and eager hearts, knowing that every step we take toward progress is a step toward a brighter, more enlightened future."

With unity in their hearts and purpose in their steps, Chilufya and his team set forth, their eyes fixed on the horizon where the pathways of progress awaited. They knew that with every policy they crafted, every innovation they embraced, and every hand they held in solidarity, they were not just building infrastructure but lighting the way to a future where learning transcends boundaries—the beacons of innovation, the torchbearers of progress.

10

Chapter 10: Criminal Justice and Public Safety

Law Enforcement Policies and Practices

"Guardians of Justice: Fortifying the Fabric of Society"

Beneath the solemn shade of the ancient baobab tree, the villagers of Kasama gathered once more, their hearts heavy with the weight of responsibility and the fervent desire for safety and security. Today, Chilufya and his team embarked on a journey to explore the crucial role of law enforcement policies and practices—the steadfast guardians tasked with upholding the rule of law and preserving the peace. With the "Building Better Communities" handbook as their beacon, they set forth to fortify the fabric of society and ensure that justice prevailed in every corner of their community.

Chilufya's voice echoed with solemnity as he addressed the assembly, underscoring the vital importance of law enforcement in maintaining order and safeguarding the rights of

158

every citizen. He spoke of the imperative to cultivate trust and transparency between law enforcement agencies and the communities they served, to ensure that justice was not just blind but compassionate, fair, and equitable for all.

To explore the realm of law enforcement policies and practices, Chilufya and his team ventured across Kasama, their hearts heavy with the burden of responsibility. Their first destination was the bustling city of Ndola, where the sirens wailed and the streets teemed with the hustle and bustle of urban life.

In Ndola, they were greeted by Superintendent Mulenga, a seasoned law enforcement officer with a steadfast commitment to serving and protecting his community. He led them through the precincts and patrol routes, where officers worked tirelessly to maintain order and respond to the needs of the public.

As they immersed themselves in the world of law enforcement, Chilufya and his team gained a deeper understanding of the challenges and complexities of the profession. Superintendent Mulenga spoke of the importance of community policing in building trust and cooperation between law enforcement officers and the communities they served, of the need for policies that prioritized accountability and professionalism, and of the role of technology in enhancing the effectiveness and efficiency of law enforcement efforts.

Next, the team journeyed to the rural communities of Southern Province, where the rhythms of life echoed the timeless wisdom of the land. There, they met with Chief Sibanda, a respected elder with a deep reverence for the rule of law and the preservation of peace.

Chief Sibanda shared tales of the challenges faced by rural

communities—limited access to law enforcement resources, vast distances and rugged terrain that made patrolling difficult, and a sense of vulnerability that threatened to erode the social fabric. He spoke of the transformative power of community engagement in preventing crime and resolving disputes, of the need for policies that empowered local leaders to work hand in hand with law enforcement agencies, and of the imperative to ensure that justice was accessible to all, regardless of geography or circumstance.

Inspired by Chief Sibanda's wisdom, Chilufya and his team returned to Kasama, their hearts heavy with the weight of responsibility. They convened a meeting under the baobab tree, inviting law enforcement officers, policymakers, and community leaders to join them on their journey to embrace law enforcement policies and practices.

Chilufya shared the stories of Ndola and Southern Province, of the bustling city and the rural communities, illustrating the urgent need for policies that prioritized community engagement, accountability, and professionalism in law enforcement efforts. He spoke of the importance of investing in training and resources for officers, of fostering partnerships between law enforcement agencies and the communities they served, and of the role of policy in ensuring that justice was not just blind but compassionate and fair for all.

One of the local elders, Mrs. Tembo, spoke of the transformative impact of effective law enforcement policies and the need to prioritize investment in community policing. "By embracing law enforcement policies and practices that prioritize accountability and professionalism, we can build a future where justice prevails and peace reigns," she declared, her voice filled with conviction.

The villagers nodded in agreement, their eyes alight with the fire of determination. They spoke of guardians of justice, of fortifying the fabric of society against the forces of chaos and disorder, and of the role of law enforcement in safeguarding the rights and freedoms of every citizen.

The local councilors pledged their support, promising to invest in law enforcement policies and practices that would lay the foundation for a more just, more secure future for Kasama. They agreed to work hand in hand with the community, ensuring that every step they took toward law enforcement was a step toward peace and prosperity for all.

As the sun dipped below the horizon, casting a golden glow over the village, Chilufya stood before the gathered multitude. "We have learned that by embracing law enforcement policies and practices that prioritize accountability, professionalism, and community engagement, we can build a future where justice prevails and peace reigns," he declared, his voice echoing through the gathering. "Let us embark on this journey together, with courage and compassion, knowing that every step we take toward justice is a step toward a brighter, safer future."

With unity in their hearts and purpose in their steps, Chilufya and his team set forth, their eyes fixed on the horizon where the guardians of justice stood vigilant, their resolve unshakeable, their commitment unwavering—the sentinels of peace, the defenders of righteousness.

Judicial Reform and Access to Justice

"Balancing Scales: A Quest for Equitable Justice"

Under the solemn shadow of the towering baobab tree, the villagers of Kasama gathered once more, their hearts heavy with the solemnity of justice and the fervent desire for fairness and equality. Today, Chilufya and his team embarked on a journey to explore the critical importance of judicial reform and access to justice—the pillars upon which the edifice of a just society stands. With the "Building Better Communities" handbook as their guide, they set forth to ensure that every individual, regardless of status or circumstance, could seek redress and find solace in the arms of justice.

Chilufya's voice resonated with gravitas as he addressed the assembly, emphasizing the indispensable role of judicial reform in upholding the rule of law and ensuring the rights of every citizen. He spoke of the imperative to cultivate a justice system that was fair, transparent, and accessible to all, to uphold the principle that justice delayed is justice denied, and to empower every individual to seek redress for grievances and wrongs.

To explore the realm of judicial reform and access to justice, Chilufya and his team ventured across Kasama, their hearts burdened by the weight of responsibility. Their first destination was the bustling city of Kitwe, where the halls of justice echoed with the solemnity of the law.

In Kitwe, they were greeted by Judge Banda, a stalwart defender of justice with a steadfast commitment to upholding the rule of law. He led them through the courtrooms and chambers, where judges and lawyers labored to administer justice and safeguard the rights of the accused.

As they immersed themselves in the world of judicial reform,

Chilufya and his team gained a deeper understanding of the challenges and complexities of the justice system. Judge Banda spoke of the importance of judicial independence and integrity in preserving the sanctity of the law, of the need for policies that promoted transparency and accountability in the judiciary, and of the imperative to ensure that justice was not just swift but equitable for all.

Next, the team journeyed to the rural communities of Luapula Province, where the rhythms of life echoed the timeless wisdom of the land. There, they met with Chief Chanda, a revered elder with a profound respect for the rule of law and the sanctity of justice.

Chief Chanda shared tales of the challenges faced by rural communities—limited access to legal resources and representation, long distances and rugged terrain that made it difficult to access courts, and a sense of disenfranchisement that threatened to erode faith in the justice system. He spoke of the transformative power of legal aid and support services in ensuring that every individual had access to justice, of the need for policies that empowered local leaders to serve as mediators and arbitrators, and of the imperative to ensure that justice was not just blind but compassionate and fair for all.

Inspired by Chief Chanda's wisdom, Chilufya and his team returned to Kasama, their hearts heavy with the burden of responsibility. They convened a meeting under the baobab tree, inviting legal experts, policymakers, and community leaders to join them on their journey to embrace judicial reform and access to justice.

Chilufya shared the stories of Kitwe and Luapula Province, of the bustling city and the rural communities, illustrating the urgent need for policies that promoted transparency, accountability, and accessibility in the justice system. He spoke of the importance of investing in legal aid and support services, of fostering partnerships between the judiciary and local leaders, and of the role of policy in ensuring that justice was not just swift but equitable for all.

One of the local elders, Mr. Simukonda, spoke of the transformative impact of access to justice and the need to prioritize investment in legal aid services. "By embracing judicial reform and ensuring access to justice for all, we can build a future where the scales of justice are balanced and the rights of every citizen are upheld," he declared, his voice filled with conviction.

The villagers nodded in agreement, their eyes alight with the fire of determination. They spoke of balancing scales, of upholding the rule of law and safeguarding the rights of the marginalized and disenfranchised, and of the role of judicial reform in ensuring that justice was not just a privilege but a right for all.

The local councilors pledged their support, promising to invest in judicial reform policies and programs that would lay the foundation for a more just, more equitable future for Kasama. They agreed to work hand in hand with the community, ensuring that every step they took toward reform was a step toward fairness and equality for all.

As the sun dipped below the horizon, casting a golden glow over the village, Chilufya stood before the gathered multitude. "We have learned that by embracing judicial reform and ensuring access to justice for all, we can build a future where the scales of justice are balanced and the rights of every citizen are upheld," he declared, his voice echoing through the gathering. "Let us embark on this journey together, with courage and compassion, knowing that every step we take toward justice is a step toward a brighter, more equitable future."

With unity in their hearts and purpose in their steps, Chilufya and his team set forth, their eyes fixed on the horizon where the scales of justice awaited, their resolve unshakeable, their commitment unwavering—the champions of fairness, the guardians of equality.

Prison and Rehabilitation Programs

"Redemption's Path: Journeying Beyond the Bars"

Under the somber boughs of the ancient baobab tree, the villagers of Kasama assembled once again, their spirits tempered by the call for compassion and the quest for rehabilitation. Today, Chilufya and his team embarked on a voyage to explore the vital role of prison and rehabilitation programs—the avenues through which redemption found its voice and second chances bloomed. With the "Building Better Communities" handbook illuminating their path, they set forth to bridge the chasm between punishment and renewal, forging a future where hope triumphed over despair.

Chilufya's voice carried on the breeze, infused with empathy and determination, as he addressed the assembly. He spoke of the imperative to view incarceration not as the end of a journey, but as the beginning of a path toward redemption and rehabilitation. He emphasized the need for prison and rehabilitation programs that sought not just to punish, but to heal, to empower, and to guide individuals back to the fold of society.

To explore the realm of prison and rehabilitation programs, Chilufya and his team traversed the breadth of Kasama, their hearts heavy with the weight of human frailty and the promise of renewal. Their first destination was the bustling city of Kabwe, where the walls of the prison echoed with the clang of iron and the whispers of forgotten dreams.

In Kabwe, they were met by Warden Kunda, a stern but compassionate guardian of justice, who led them through the labyrinthine corridors and dimly lit cells of the prison. He spoke of the challenges faced by inmates—poverty, addiction, mental illness—and the transformative power of education, counseling, and vocational training in breaking the cycle of crime and despair.

As they immersed themselves in the world behind bars, Chilufya and his team gained a deeper understanding of the complexities of rehabilitation. Warden Kunda spoke of the need for policies that prioritized education and skills development, that provided inmates with the tools they needed to rebuild their lives and contribute meaningfully to society upon their release.

Next, the team journeyed to the rural communities of Eastern Province, where the rhythms of life echoed the timeless wisdom of the land. There, they met with Pastor Mulenga, a beacon of hope in a sea of darkness, who ministered to the spiritual needs of inmates and advocated tirelessly for their redemption.

Pastor Mulenga shared tales of transformation—of inmates who had found solace in faith, who had turned away from lives of crime and violence and embraced a path of peace and renewal. He spoke of the importance of counseling and support services in addressing the underlying trauma and addiction that often fueled criminal behavior, of the need for policies that recognized the humanity and potential for change in every individual, no matter how lost or broken.

Inspired by Pastor Mulenga's compassion, Chilufya and his team returned to Kasama, their hearts heavy with the weight of responsibility. They convened a meeting under the baobab tree, inviting prison officials, counselors, and community leaders to join them on their journey to embrace prison and rehabilitation programs.

Chilufya shared the stories of Kabwe and Eastern Province, of the bustling city and the rural communities, illustrating the urgent need for policies that prioritized rehabilitation and reintegration into society. He spoke of the importance of investing in education, counseling, and vocational training, of providing inmates with the tools they needed to rebuild their lives and contribute meaningfully to society upon their release.

One of the former inmates, Mr. Mwamba, spoke of the transformative impact of rehabilitation programs and the need to prioritize investment in reintegration services. "By embracing prison and rehabilitation programs that seek to heal and empower, we can build a future where second chances are not just a dream but a reality," he declared, his voice filled with conviction.

The villagers nodded in agreement, their eyes alight with the fire of hope. They spoke of redemption's path, of journeying beyond the bars to a future where forgiveness triumphed over judgment, where compassion overcame condemnation, and where every individual had the opportunity to find their way back to the light.

The local councilors pledged their support, promising to invest in prison and rehabilitation programs that would lay the foundation for a more just, more compassionate future for Kasama. They agreed to work hand in hand with the community, ensuring that every step they took toward rehabilitation was a step toward healing and renewal for all.

As the sun dipped below the horizon, casting a golden glow over the village, Chilufya stood before the gathered multitude. "We have learned that by embracing prison and rehabilitation programs that seek to heal and empower, we can build a future where second chances are not just a dream but a reality," he declared, his voice echoing through the gathering. "Let us embark on this journey together, with compassion and conviction, knowing that every step we take toward redemption is a step toward a brighter, more hopeful future."

With unity in their hearts and purpose in their steps, Chilufya and his team set forth, their eyes fixed on the horizon where redemption's path awaited, their resolve unshakeable, their commitment unwavering—the architects of renewal, the stewards of second chances.

Crime Prevention Strategies

"Shield of Hope: Crafting a Crime-Free Tomorrow"

Beneath the ancient, sprawling baobab tree, the villagers of Kasama gathered once more, their hearts united by the common goal of safeguarding their community from the specter of crime. Today, Chilufya and his team embarked on a journey to explore the critical importance of crime prevention strategies—the shield that protected their way of life and nurtured a safe, thriving community. With the "Building Better Communities" handbook as their guide, they set forth to design a future where vigilance and unity prevailed over fear and disorder.

Chilufya's voice rang clear and confident as he addressed the assembly, highlighting the urgent need for proactive measures to prevent crime before it took root. He spoke of the imperative to foster a sense of security and trust within the community, to empower individuals with the tools and knowledge to protect themselves and their neighbors, and to cultivate an environment where crime could not flourish.

To explore the realm of crime prevention strategies, Chilufya and his team ventured across Kasama, their hearts heavy with the responsibility to protect and the promise of safety. Their first destination was the vibrant city of Lusaka, where the streets buzzed with the hum of daily life and the ever-present challenge of urban crime.

In Lusaka, they met with Inspector Chibwe, a dedicated police officer committed to innovative crime prevention. He led them through the bustling marketplaces and quiet residential neighborhoods, illustrating the diverse strategies employed to deter criminal activity. Inspector Chibwe spoke of community policing, where officers worked closely with residents to build trust and gather intelligence, and of the importance of visibility and presence in high-crime areas.

As they delved deeper into the intricacies of crime prevention, Chilufya and his team gained a profound understanding of the multi-faceted approach required to tackle crime. Inspector Chibwe highlighted the role of education and awareness campaigns in informing the public about safety measures, the importance of neighborhood watch programs in fostering a collective sense of responsibility, and the need for infrastructure improvements, such as street lighting and secure housing, to reduce opportunities for crime.

Next, the team journeyed to the rural communities of Western Province, where the rhythms of life were slower, but the challenges of crime prevention were no less pressing. There, they met with Chief Mwansa, a revered elder who had implemented traditional methods of community vigilance and justice.

Chief Mwansa shared stories of the challenges faced by rural communities—cattle rustling, petty theft, and the occasional violent crime. He spoke of the importance of involving the entire community in crime prevention efforts, of leveraging traditional customs and practices to maintain order, and of the need for policies that supported rural infrastructure development to enhance security.

Inspired by Chief Mwansa's wisdom and Inspector Chibwe's innovative approach, Chilufya and his team returned to Kasama, their hearts heavy with the responsibility to protect their community. They convened a meeting under the baobab tree, inviting law enforcement officers, policymakers, and community leaders to join them on their journey to embrace crime prevention strategies.

Chilufya shared the stories of Lusaka and Western Province, of the bustling city and the rural communities, illustrating the urgent need for a comprehensive, multi-faceted approach to crime prevention. He spoke of the importance of investing in community policing, education and awareness campaigns, neighborhood watch programs, and infrastructure improvements to create a safer, more secure environment for all.

One of the local youths, Temwani, spoke passionately about the transformative impact of crime prevention efforts and the need to involve young people in these initiatives. "By embracing crime prevention strategies that empower and protect, we can build a future where our streets are safe, and our communities thrive," she declared, her voice filled with determination.

The villagers nodded in agreement, their eyes shining with the fire of resolve. They spoke of the shield of hope, of crafting a crime-free tomorrow through vigilance, unity, and proactive measures. They acknowledged the role of each individual in maintaining the safety and security of their community and pledged to work together to implement the strategies they had learned.

The local councilors pledged their support, promising to invest in crime prevention programs and policies that would lay the foundation for a more secure future for Kasama. They agreed to work hand in hand with the community, ensuring that every step they took toward prevention was a step toward a safer, more prosperous tomorrow.

As the sun set, casting a golden glow over the village, Chilufya stood before the gathered multitude. "We have learned that by embracing crime prevention strategies that empower and protect, we can build a future where our streets are safe, and our communities thrive," he declared, his voice echoing through the gathering. "Let us embark on this journey together, with vigilance and unity, knowing that every step we take toward prevention is a step toward a brighter, more secure future."

With unity in their hearts and purpose in their steps, Chilufya and his team set forth, their eyes fixed on the horizon where the shield of hope awaited, their resolve unshakeable, their commitment unwavering—the architects of safety, the guardians of tomorrow.

Restorative Justice Approaches

"Healing the Wounds: Embracing Restorative Justice"

As the sun dipped below the horizon, casting a golden glow over the village of Kasama, the villagers gathered once more under the ancient baobab tree. The air was thick with anticipation as Chilufya and his team prepared to explore a new dimension of justice—restorative justice, a path that sought to heal rather than punish, to mend the fabric of their community by addressing the harm caused by crime. Guided by the "Building Better Communities" handbook, they embarked on a journey to understand the transformative power of reconciliation and restoration.

Chilufya's voice was gentle yet firm as he addressed the assembly, emphasizing the vital need for a justice system that went beyond retribution to focus on healing and restoration. He spoke of the principles of restorative justice, which sought to involve victims, offenders, and the community in a process of dialogue and reconciliation, aiming to repair the harm caused by crime and restore relationships.

To delve into the world of restorative justice, Chilufya and his team journeyed across Kasama, their hearts filled with the hope of finding new ways to address crime. Their first destination was the bustling city of Livingstone, where they visited the Restorative Justice Center, a pioneering institution dedicated to implementing restorative practices.

In Livingstone, they met with Ms. Mwila, the director of the center, who guided them through the principles and practices of restorative justice. She shared stories of mediation sessions where victims and offenders came together to discuss the impact of the crime, to seek understanding, and to find ways to make amends. Ms. Mwila emphasized the importance of empathy, communication, and community involvement in the restorative justice process.

As they immersed themselves in the philosophy of restorative justice, Chilufya and his team witnessed powerful examples of transformation. They saw how offenders, confronted with the human impact of their actions, expressed genuine remorse and took steps to make amends. They saw victims, once burdened with anger and pain, finding a sense of closure and healing through dialogue and reconciliation.

Next, the team journeyed to the rural communities of Northern Province, where the traditions of communal living and collective responsibility echoed the principles of restorative justice. There, they met with Elder Nkandu, a wise leader who had long practiced traditional forms of conflict resolution.

Elder Nkandu shared stories of the village assemblies, where community members gathered to resolve disputes, to discuss the impact of wrongdoing, and to find ways to restore harmony. He spoke of the importance of involving the entire community in the justice process, of the need for policies that supported restorative practices, and of the power of forgiveness and reconciliation in healing the wounds of crime.

Inspired by the wisdom of Elder Nkandu and the innovative practices of the Restorative Justice Center, Chilufya and his team returned to Kasama, their hearts heavy with the responsibility to bring about change. They convened a meeting under the baobab tree, inviting mediators, legal experts, and community leaders to join them on their journey to embrace restorative justice approaches.

Chilufya shared the stories of Livingstone and Northern Province, illustrating the urgent need for a justice system that prioritized healing and restoration. He spoke of the importance of investing in restorative justice programs, of training mediators to facilitate dialogue and reconciliation, and of involving the community in the process of healing and restoration.

One of the victims of a recent theft, Mrs. Banda, shared her story of participating in a restorative justice session. She spoke of the profound impact of hearing the offender's remorse, of the sense of closure she found through the process, and of the hope that restorative justice could bring to others. "By embracing restorative justice approaches, we can heal our wounds and build a community where understanding and forgiveness prevail," she declared, her voice filled with conviction.

The villagers nodded in agreement, their eyes alight with the fire of hope. They spoke of healing the wounds of crime, of mending the fabric of their community through empathy, dialogue, and reconciliation. They acknowledged the role of each individual in the restorative justice process and pledged to work together to implement the practices they had learned.

The local councilors pledged their support, promising to invest in restorative justice programs and policies that would lay the foundation for a more harmonious future for Kasama. They agreed to work hand in hand with the community, ensuring that every step they took toward restoration was a step toward healing and renewal for all.

As the stars began to twinkle in the night sky, casting a serene glow over the village, Chilufya stood before the gathered multitude. "We have learned that by embracing restorative justice approaches, we can heal our wounds and build a community where understanding and forgiveness prevail," he declared, his voice echoing through the gathering. "Let us embark on this journey together, with empathy and hope, knowing that every step we take toward restoration is a step toward a brighter, more harmonious future."

With unity in their hearts and purpose in their steps, Chilufya and his team set forth, their eyes fixed on the horizon where the promise of healing awaited, their resolve unshakeable, their commitment unwavering—the architects of restoration, the stewards of reconciliation.

Community Policing and Engagement

"Guardians of Trust: Community Policing in Action"

Under the spreading branches of the ancient baobab tree, the villagers of Kasama gathered once more, their hearts united by a shared vision of a safer, more connected community. Chilufya and his team prepared to delve into the heart of community policing and engagement—a strategy that fostered trust and cooperation between the police and the people they served. With the "Building Better Communities" handbook as their guide, they embarked on a journey to create a future where safety was a shared responsibility, and trust was the foundation of their community.

Chilufya's voice carried a sense of optimism and determination as he addressed the assembly, highlighting the critical role of community policing in creating a secure and cohesive society. He spoke of the principles of community policing, which emphasized building relationships between law enforcement and community members, fostering mutual trust, and working together to address the root causes of crime.

To explore the world of community policing, Chilufya and his team traveled across Kasama, their hearts filled with the hope of forging stronger bonds between the police and the community. Their first destination was the bustling town of Kitwe, where they visited a police station renowned for its successful community policing initiatives.

In Kitwe, they met with Officer Banda, a dedicated community policing officer who had built strong connections with local residents. He led them through the neighborhoods, introducing them to community members who shared stories of collaboration and mutual support. Officer Banda spoke of the importance of regular patrols, community meetings, and open communication channels in building trust and fostering a sense of security.

As they immersed themselves in the principles of community policing, Chilufya and his team witnessed firsthand the transformative power of engagement. They saw how officers, by being present and approachable, became trusted figures in the community. They saw residents actively participating in safety initiatives, from neighborhood watch programs to youth mentorship schemes, all contributing to a more secure environment.

Next, the team journeyed to the rural areas of Southern Province, where the bonds of community were deeply rooted in traditional values. There, they met with Chief Chikondi, a respected leader who had successfully integrated community policing practices with traditional governance.

Chief Chikondi shared stories of how community policing had helped address issues such as cattle theft and domestic violence. He emphasized the importance of involving traditional leaders in policing efforts, of leveraging cultural practices to maintain order, and of the need for policies that supported rural policing initiatives. He spoke of the role of community meetings, where residents and police officers discussed safety concerns and collaborated on solutions.

Inspired by Officer Banda's dedication and Chief Chikondi's wisdom, Chilufya and his team returned to Kasama, their hearts filled with a renewed sense of purpose. They convened a meeting under the baobab tree, inviting police officers, community leaders, and residents to join them on their journey to embrace community policing and engagement.

Chilufya shared the stories of Kitwe and Southern Province, illustrating the urgent need for a policing model that prioritized relationship-building and collaboration. He spoke of the importance of investing in community policing programs, of training officers to engage with residents effectively, and of involving the community in safety initiatives.

One of the local elders, Mr. Mutale, shared his experience of working with community policing officers to address issues in his neighborhood. He spoke of the trust that had been built, the reduction in crime, and the sense of empowerment felt by residents. "By embracing community policing and engagement, we can build a future where trust and cooperation are the cornerstones of our safety," he declared, his voice filled with conviction.

The villagers nodded in agreement, their eyes shining with hope and determination. They spoke of becoming guardians of trust, of creating a community where safety was a shared responsibility, and where the bonds between police and residents were strong and unbreakable. They acknowledged the role of each individual in the success of community policing and pledged to work together to implement the practices they had learned.

The local councilors pledged their support, promising to invest in community policing programs and policies that would lay the foundation for a more secure and connected future for Kasama. They agreed to work hand in hand with the community, ensuring that every step they took toward engagement was a step toward a safer, more cohesive society.

As the sun set, casting a golden glow over the village, Chilufya stood before the gathered multitude. "We have learned that by embracing community policing and engagement, we can build a future where trust and cooperation are the cornerstones of our safety," he declared, his voice echoing through the gathering. "Let us embark on this journey together, with trust and determination, knowing that every step we take toward engagement is a step toward a brighter, more secure future."

With unity in their hearts and purpose in their steps, Chilufya and his team set forth, their eyes fixed on the horizon where the promise of trust awaited, their resolve unshakeable, their commitment unwavering—the architects of engagement, the guardians of trust.

11

Chapter 11: Immigration Policy and Integration

Immigration Reform and Border Security

"Bridges of Unity: Immigration Policy and Community Integration"

The warm, welcoming village of Kasama gathered under the ancient baobab tree, ready to explore a new chapter in their journey of building better communities. Today, Chilufya and his team would delve into the complex world of immigration policy and integration. Their goal was to understand the balance between immigration reform and border security, ensuring that their community remained safe while also welcoming those who sought a better life within their borders. Guided by the "Building Better Communities" handbook, they set out to explore how they could build bridges of unity in the face of diverse challenges.

Chilufya's voice carried a tone of empathy and determination as he addressed the assembly, highlighting the importance of thoughtful immigration reform and robust border security. He spoke of the need to protect the community while also providing a safe haven for those fleeing hardship and seeking new opportunities. He emphasized the dual goals of security and compassion, urging the community to consider both as they shaped their policies.

To gain a comprehensive understanding of immigration reform and border security, Chilufya and his team traveled across Kasama and beyond. Their first destination was the bustling border town of Nakonde, a key entry point for many migrants. Here, they met with Immigration Officer Mwansa, who managed the delicate balance between welcoming newcomers and maintaining security.

Officer Mwansa explained the challenges faced at the border, including the need to prevent illegal activities while also ensuring that genuine asylum seekers and immigrants were treated with dignity and respect. He highlighted the importance of clear, fair immigration policies and the need for adequate resources to support both enforcement and humanitarian efforts.

Chilufya and his team observed the rigorous security measures in place at the border, including patrols, checkpoints, and technology to monitor movement. They also witnessed the humane treatment of those seeking entry, with facilities to provide food, shelter, and medical care. The importance of a well-resourced and balanced approach to border security became evident, as did the need for continuous reform to address emerging challenges.

Next, the team traveled to the vibrant city of Lusaka, where they visited a community center dedicated to supporting immigrants and refugees. There, they met with Mrs. Phiri, the center's director, who passionately spoke about the integration challenges faced by newcomers and the role of community support in their successful adaptation.

Mrs. Phiri shared stories of immigrants who had fled conflict and economic hardship, arriving in Zambia with hopes of rebuilding their lives. She emphasized the importance of comprehensive immigration reform that provided clear pathways to legal status and integration programs that included language classes, job training, and cultural orientation.

Inspired by Officer Mwansa's commitment and Mrs. Phiri's compassion, Chilufya and his team returned to Kasama with a deeper understanding of the complexities of immigration policy. They convened a meeting under the baobab tree, inviting immigration officers, community leaders, and residents to join them in shaping their approach to immigration reform and border security.

Chilufya shared the lessons from Nakonde and Lusaka, illustrating the need for a balanced approach that prioritized both security and compassion. He spoke of the importance of clear immigration policies, the provision of resources for border security, and the establishment of programs to support the integration of immigrants into the community.

One of the local teachers, Mr. Kabwe, shared his experience of teaching children from immigrant families. He spoke of the challenges they faced, from language barriers to cultural differences, and the incredible potential they had to contribute to the community. "By embracing thoughtful immigration reform and ensuring robust border security, we can build bridges of unity and create a community where everyone has the opportunity to thrive," he declared, his voice filled with hope.

The villagers nodded in agreement, their eyes shining with resolve. They spoke of building bridges of unity, of creating a community that was both safe and welcoming. They acknowledged the role of each individual in supporting immigrants and ensuring security, pledging to work together to implement the policies they had learned.

The local councilors pledged their support, promising to invest in immigration reform and border security measures that would lay the foundation for a safer, more inclusive future for Kasama. They agreed to work hand in hand with the community, ensuring that every step they took toward reform and security was a step toward a more united, compassionate society.

As the sun set, casting a golden glow over the village, Chilufya stood before the gathered multitude. "We have learned that by embracing thoughtful immigration reform and ensuring robust border security, we can build bridges of unity and create a community where everyone has the opportunity to thrive," he declared, his voice echoing through the gathering. "Let us embark on this journey together, with empathy and determination, knowing that every step we take toward reform and security is a step toward a brighter, more inclusive future."

With unity in their hearts and purpose in their steps, Chilufya and his team set forth, their eyes fixed on the horizon where the promise of unity awaited, their resolve unshakeable, their commitment unwavering—the architects of reform, the builders of bridges.

Refugee Resettlement and Asylum Policies

"Safe Haven: Navigating Refugee Resettlement and Asylum Policies"

The village of Kasama gathered once more under the ancient baobab tree, a place that had become a symbol of their commitment to building better communities. Chilufya and his team were ready to explore another critical aspect of immigration policy—refugee resettlement and asylum policies. Guided by the "Building Better Communities" handbook, they sought to understand how they could offer a safe haven to those fleeing persecution and conflict, integrating them into their community with compassion and support.

Chilufya's voice was filled with empathy and resolve as he addressed the assembly, highlighting the importance of providing refuge to those in need while ensuring their successful integration into the community. He spoke of the principles of refugee resettlement and asylum, emphasizing the need for policies that protected human rights and offered opportunities for new beginnings.

To gain a comprehensive understanding of refugee resettlement and asylum policies, Chilufya and his team traveled to various parts of Zambia, seeking insights from places where these policies were actively implemented. Their first destination was the Meheba Refugee Settlement in the North-Western Province, a place that had provided sanctuary to thousands of refugees over the years.

At Meheba, they met with Ms. Kalaba, the settlement manager, who guided them through the process of resettlement. She explained the challenges faced by refugees upon arrival, including trauma, loss, and the need for basic necessities. Ms. Kalaba highlighted the importance of providing immediate support such as food, shelter, and medical care, followed by programs aimed at fostering self-sufficiency, such as vocational training and educational opportunities.

Chilufya and his team were deeply moved by the resilience of the refugees they met. They listened to stories of hardship and hope, of families who had fled violence and persecution, and of their dreams for a new life in Zambia. The importance of comprehensive asylum policies became clear, as did the need for community involvement in supporting resettlement efforts.

Next, the team traveled to Lusaka, where they visited the Refugee Services Office, an organization dedicated to assisting asylum seekers and refugees in urban areas. There, they met with Mr. Nkomo, the director, who spoke about the complexities of asylum policies and the need for a fair and efficient asylum process.

Mr. Nkomo shared stories of individuals who had sought asylum in Zambia, highlighting the legal and bureaucratic hurdles they faced. He emphasized the importance of clear, humane asylum policies that protected the rights of asylum seekers and provided a pathway to legal status and integration. He also spoke of the role of community support networks in helping asylum seekers adapt to their new environment.

Inspired by Ms. Kalaba's dedication and Mr. Nkomo's advocacy, Chilufya and his team returned to Kasama, their hearts filled with a deeper understanding of the challenges and opportunities in refugee resettlement and asylum policies. They convened a meeting under the baobab tree, inviting community leaders, residents, and representatives from refugee organizations to join them in shaping their approach to providing a safe haven for refugees.

Chilufya shared the lessons from Meheba and Lusaka, illustrating the need for policies that prioritized both protection and integration. He spoke of the importance of immediate support for refugees, the provision of educational and vocational programs, and the establishment of clear pathways to legal status for asylum seekers.

One of the local health workers, Ms. Tembo, shared her experience of providing medical care to refugee families. She spoke of the trauma they had endured, the health challenges they faced, and the incredible strength they demonstrated. "By embracing compassionate refugee resettlement and asylum policies, we can offer a safe haven and help build a future where everyone has the opportunity to thrive," she declared, her voice filled with empathy.

The villagers nodded in agreement, their eyes shining with compassion and determination. They spoke of creating a community where refugees were welcomed and supported, where their rights were protected, and their contributions valued. They acknowledged the role of each individual in the resettlement process and pledged to work together to implement the policies they had learned.

The local councilors pledged their support, promising to invest in refugee resettlement programs and asylum policies that would lay the foundation for a more inclusive and supportive future for Kasama. They agreed to work hand in hand with the community, ensuring that every step they took toward providing a safe haven was a step toward a more united, compassionate society.

As the sun set, casting a golden glow over the village, Chilufya stood before the gathered multitude. "We have learned that by embracing compassionate refugee resettlement and asylum policies, we can offer a safe haven and help build a future where everyone has the opportunity to thrive," he declared, his voice echoing through the gathering. "Let us embark on this journey together, with compassion and determination, knowing that every step we take toward providing refuge is a step toward a brighter, more inclusive future."

With unity in their hearts and purpose in their steps, Chilufya and his team set forth, their eyes fixed on the horizon where the promise of sanctuary awaited, their resolve unshakeable, their commitment unwavering—the architects of refuge, the builders of safe havens.

Integration Programs for Newcomers

"Welcoming Hearts: Integration Programs for Newcomers"

Under the shade of the ancient baobab tree, the villagers of Kasama gathered once more, united by their shared vision of a community where every individual could thrive. Today, Chilufya and his team were ready to explore the final subpoint of immigration policy—integration programs for newcomers. Guided by the "Building Better Communities" handbook, they sought to understand how they could create inclusive and supportive programs to help immigrants and refugees adapt to their new lives in Kasama.

Chilufya's voice was filled with warmth and determination as he addressed the assembly, highlighting the importance of helping newcomers integrate into the community. He spoke of the challenges faced by immigrants and refugees as they adjusted to new cultures, languages, and systems. He emphasized the need for comprehensive integration programs that would provide them with the tools and support necessary to succeed.

To gain a deeper understanding of effective integration programs, Chilufya and his team traveled across Kasama and beyond. Their first destination was the city of Ndola, where they visited a successful immigrant integration center known for its innovative programs. There, they met with Mrs. Mumba, the center's director, who had dedicated her life to helping newcomers build successful lives in Zambia.

Mrs. Mumba explained the various integration programs offered at the center, including language classes, job training, cultural orientation sessions, and mentorship programs. She emphasized the importance of creating a welcoming environment where newcomers felt supported and valued. Chilufya and his team observed classes where immigrants were learning Bemba and English, workshops where they were acquiring new skills, and community events where they were connecting with local residents.

Chilufya and his team were inspired by the resilience and determination of the immigrants they met. They listened to stories of challenges overcome and dreams pursued, gaining insight into the critical role that integration programs played in their success. The importance of a holistic approach to integration became clear, as did the need for community involvement in supporting newcomers.

Next, the team traveled to the bustling town of Livingstone, where they visited a community-led initiative that paired local families with immigrant families to help them navigate their new environment. There, they met with Mr. Ndlovu, a community leader who had spearheaded the program, and several participating families.

Mr. Ndlovu shared stories of how the program had fostered strong bonds between locals and newcomers, helping immigrants feel more at home while enriching the community with diverse perspectives. He spoke of the mutual benefits of these relationships, from cultural exchange to shared experiences that strengthened the community fabric.

Inspired by Mrs. Mumba's dedication and Mr. Ndlovu's community spirit, Chilufya and his team returned to Kasama, their hearts filled with a renewed sense of purpose. They convened a meeting under the baobab tree, inviting community leaders, residents, and representatives from local organizations to join them in discussing integration programs for newcomers.

Chilufya shared the lessons from Ndola and Livingstone, illustrating the need for comprehensive and inclusive integration programs. He spoke of the importance of language and job training, cultural orientation, and mentorship, emphasizing the role of the community in supporting these initiatives.

One of the local teachers, Ms. Banda, shared her experience of teaching children from immigrant families. She spoke of the language barriers they faced, the cultural differences they navigated, and the incredible potential they exhibited. "By embracing comprehensive integration programs, we can create a community where every individual, regardless of their background, has the opportunity to thrive," she declared, her voice filled with hope.

The villagers nodded in agreement, their eyes shining with determination. They spoke of creating a welcoming community, where newcomers were supported and valued.

They acknowledged the role of each individual in the success of integration programs and pledged to work together to implement the initiatives they had learned.

The local councilors pledged their support, promising to invest in integration programs that would lay the foundation for a more inclusive and supportive future for Kasama. They agreed to work hand in hand with the community, ensuring that every step they took toward integration was a step toward a more united, compassionate society.

As the sun set, casting a golden glow over the village, Chilufya stood before the gathered multitude. "We have learned that by embracing comprehensive integration programs, we can create a community where every individual has the opportunity to thrive," he declared, his voice echoing through the gathering. "Let us embark on this journey together, with empathy and determination, knowing that every step we take toward integration is a step toward a brighter, more inclusive future."

With unity in their hearts and purpose in their steps, Chilufya and his team set forth, their eyes fixed on the horizon where the promise of belonging awaited, their resolve unshakeable, their commitment unwavering—the architects of integration, the builders of welcoming hearts.

Citizenship and Neutralization Processes

"Becoming One: Citizenship and Naturalization Processes"

As the sun rose over Kasama, casting its first light on the ancient baobab tree, the villagers gathered once more. Today, Chilufya and his team were ready to explore the final aspect of their journey on immigration policy—citizenship and naturalization processes. Guided by the "Building Better Communities" handbook, they sought to understand how they could facilitate the journey from newcomer to citizen, ensuring that everyone who called Kasama home felt a true sense of belonging.

Chilufya's voice resonated with purpose as he addressed the assembly. He emphasized the significance of citizenship and naturalization, explaining that these processes not only provided legal recognition but also fostered a deeper sense of identity and belonging. "Becoming a citizen means more than just holding a passport; it means being part of the fabric of our community," he declared.

To gain a comprehensive understanding of the citizenship and naturalization processes, Chilufya and his team traveled across Zambia, seeking insights from those who had navigated these journeys. Their first destination was the capital city of Lusaka, where they visited the Department of National Registration, Passport, and Citizenship. There, they met with Mr. Chanda, the head of the citizenship division, who explained the legal and procedural aspects of naturalization.

Mr. Chanda outlined the steps involved in applying for citizenship, including residency requirements, language proficiency, and civic knowledge. He emphasized the importance of making the process accessible and transparent to ensure that deserving individuals could successfully become citizens. Chilufya and his team observed the application process and spoke with applicants about their experiences, gaining valuable insights into the challenges and aspirations of those seeking citizenship.

Chilufya and his team were inspired by the determination

of the applicants they met. They listened to stories of perseverance and hope, of individuals who had worked tirelessly to meet the requirements for naturalization. The importance of clear, fair, and supportive citizenship processes became evident, as did the need for community involvement in welcoming new citizens.

Next, the team traveled to the city of Kitwe, where they visited a local NGO that provided assistance to immigrants navigating the naturalization process. There, they met with Ms. Zulu, the program director, who passionately spoke about the role of community support in helping individuals achieve citizenship.

Ms. Zulu shared stories of immigrants who had successfully become citizens, highlighting the impact of mentorship, legal assistance, and educational programs. She emphasized the importance of creating a welcoming environment where newcomers felt supported throughout their journey to citizenship. Chilufya and his team observed workshops where immigrants learned about Zambian history and culture, and mentorship sessions where experienced citizens guided applicants through the naturalization process.

Inspired by Mr. Chanda's expertise and Ms. Zulu's dedication, Chilufya and his team returned to Kasama, their hearts filled with a renewed sense of purpose. They convened a meeting under the baobab tree, inviting community leaders, residents, and representatives from local organizations to join them in discussing citizenship and naturalization processes.

Chilufya shared the lessons from Lusaka and Kitwe, illustrating the need for clear and supportive citizenship processes. He spoke of the importance of residency requirements, language proficiency, and civic knowledge, and emphasized the role of the community in supporting these initiatives.

One of the local elders, Mr. Phiri, shared his experience of guiding a family through the naturalization process. He spoke of the pride they felt upon receiving their citizenship, and the deep connection they developed with the community. "By embracing comprehensive citizenship and naturalization processes, we can create a community where everyone feels a true sense of belonging," he declared, his voice filled with warmth.

The villagers nodded in agreement, their eyes shining with determination. They spoke of creating a community where newcomers were welcomed and supported, where their journey to citizenship was met with guidance and encouragement. They acknowledged the role of each individual in the naturalization process and pledged to work together to implement the policies they had learned.

The local councilors pledged their support, promising to invest in citizenship and naturalization programs that would lay the foundation for a more inclusive and supportive future for Kasama. They agreed to work hand in hand with the community, ensuring that every step they took toward citizenship was a step toward a more united, compassionate society.

As the sun set, casting a golden glow over the village, Chilufya stood before the gathered multitude. "We have learned that by embracing comprehensive citizenship and naturalization processes, we can create a community where everyone feels a true sense of belonging," he declared, his voice echoing through the gathering. "Let us embark on this journey together, with empathy and determination, knowing that every step we take toward citizenship is a step toward a brighter, more inclusive future."

With unity in their hearts and purpose in their steps, Chilufya and his team set forth, their eyes fixed on the horizon where the promise of belonging awaited, their resolve unshakeable, their commitment unwavering—the architects of citizenship, the builders of unity.

Addressing Xenophobia and Discrimination

"United Front: Addressing Xenophobia and Discrimination"

As dusk fell over Kasama, the ancient baobab tree stood as a sentinel to the village's commitment to unity and progress. Chilufya and his team gathered once more to tackle a crucial and sensitive aspect of their immigration policy journey— addressing xenophobia and discrimination. Guided by the "Building Better Communities" handbook, they were determined to foster an environment where every individual, regardless of origin, felt safe and valued.

Chilufya's voice carried a somber yet resolute tone as he addressed the assembly. "Xenophobia and discrimination threaten the very foundation of our community," he began. "We must confront these issues head-on and build a culture of acceptance and respect."

To better understand how to address xenophobia and discrimination, Chilufya and his team embarked on a journey across Zambia, seeking wisdom from communities that had successfully combated these challenges. Their first stop was the vibrant city of Lusaka, where they visited an organization called Ubuntu Zambia, dedicated to promoting social harmony and combating xenophobia.

At Ubuntu Zambia, they met with Ms. Mwansa, the founder, who shared her insights on fostering inclusion and respect. She spoke of educational campaigns, community dialogues, and support networks that had proven effective in addressing xenophobia. Chilufya and his team observed workshops where locals and immigrants shared their stories, breaking down stereotypes and building mutual understanding.

Chilufya and his team were inspired by the transformative power of these conversations. They listened to stories of fear and prejudice overcome by empathy and respect, realizing the importance of open dialogue and education in combating xenophobia. The need for proactive community engagement became clear, as did the role of leaders in setting a tone of inclusion.

Next, the team traveled to the culturally diverse town of Livingstone, where they visited a youth center known for its anti-discrimination initiatives. There, they met with Mr. Banda, a youth leader who had organized numerous campaigns to promote inclusivity among the younger generation.

Mr. Banda shared stories of how the youth center had become a beacon of hope, fostering a sense of belonging and acceptance among young people from diverse backgrounds. He emphasized the importance of involving youth in these efforts, as they were the future leaders and change-makers of their communities. Chilufya and his team observed interactive activities where youths learned about different cultures and worked together on community projects.

Inspired by Ms. Mwansa's dedication and Mr. Banda's youthful energy, Chilufya and his team returned to Kasama, their hearts filled with a renewed sense of urgency and purpose. They convened a meeting under the baobab tree, inviting community leaders, residents, and representatives from local organizations to join them in discussing strategies to address xenophobia and discrimination.

Chilufya shared the lessons from Lusaka and Livingstone, illustrating the need for proactive and inclusive approaches. He spoke of the importance of educational campaigns, community dialogues, and youth involvement, emphasizing the role of the community in fostering a culture of acceptance and respect.

One of the local educators, Mrs. Kapata, shared her experience of teaching students from diverse backgrounds. She spoke of the importance of creating a safe and inclusive learning environment where every child felt valued and respected. "By addressing xenophobia and discrimination, we can build a community where every individual is free to contribute their unique strengths," she declared, her voice filled with conviction.

The villagers nodded in agreement, their eyes shining with determination. They spoke of creating a community where diversity was celebrated, and everyone was treated with dignity and respect. They acknowledged the role of each individual in combating xenophobia and pledged to work together to implement the initiatives they had learned.

The local councilors pledged their support, promising to invest in anti-xenophobia campaigns and educational programs that would lay the foundation for a more inclusive and supportive future for Kasama. They agreed to work hand in hand with the community, ensuring that every step they took toward inclusivity was a step toward a more united, compassionate society.

As the moon rose, casting a silvery light over the village,

Chilufya stood before the gathered multitude. "We have learned that by addressing xenophobia and discrimination, we can build a community where every individual is free to contribute their unique strengths," he declared, his voice echoing through the gathering. "Let us embark on this journey together, with empathy and determination, knowing that every step we take toward inclusivity is a step toward a brighter, more united future."

With unity in their hearts and purpose in their steps, Chilufya and his team set forth, their eyes fixed on the horizon where the promise of acceptance awaited, their resolve unshakeable, their commitment unwavering—the architects of inclusivity, the builders of unity.

Economic Impact of Immigration

"Building Prosperity: The Economic Impact of Immigration"

As the morning sun illuminated the village of Kasama, casting a golden glow over the ancient baobab tree, the community gathered once more. Today, Chilufya and his team were set to explore a crucial aspect of their immigration policy journey—the economic impact of immigration. Guided by the "Building Better Communities" handbook, they aimed to understand how immigration could drive economic growth and prosperity for all.

Chilufya began the discussion with a hopeful tone. "Immigration, when managed well, can bring significant economic benefits to our community," he said. "Let's explore how we can harness this potential to build a stronger, more prosperous Kasama."

To gain insights into the economic impact of immigration, Chilufya and his team traveled across Zambia, visiting communities that had successfully integrated immigrants into their local economies. Their first stop was the thriving commercial hub of Ndola, where they visited a market known for its diversity and economic vibrancy.

In Ndola, they met with Mr. Kunda, a market manager who explained how the influx of immigrants had revitalized the local economy. He spoke of new businesses, increased trade, and the introduction of diverse products and services. Chilufya and his team observed bustling market stalls run by immigrants and locals alike, each contributing to the economic tapestry of the community.

Chilufya and his team were inspired by the stories of entrepreneurial immigrants who had set up successful businesses, creating jobs and stimulating economic activity. They listened to stories of collaboration and mutual benefit, realizing the importance of supporting immigrant entrepreneurs and integrating them into the local economy.

Next, the team traveled to the agricultural town of Choma, where they visited a cooperative that included both local farmers and immigrant workers. There, they met with Mrs. Mwale, the cooperative's chairperson, who passionately spoke about the positive impact of immigrant labor on local agriculture.

Mrs. Mwale shared how immigrant workers had filled crucial labor shortages, boosting productivity and enabling the cooperative to expand its operations. She emphasized the importance of fair treatment and integration, ensuring that immigrant workers felt valued and part of the community. Chilufya and his team observed the cooperative in action, witnessing the harmonious collaboration between locals and immigrants.

Inspired by Mr. Kunda's insights and Mrs. Mwale's leadership, Chilufya and his team returned to Kasama with a renewed sense of purpose. They convened a meeting under the baobab tree, inviting community leaders, residents, and local business owners to join them in discussing the economic impact of immigration.

Chilufya shared the lessons from Ndola and Choma, illustrating the potential for economic growth through immigration. He spoke of the importance of supporting immigrant entrepreneurs, integrating immigrant workers, and fostering an environment where everyone could contribute to the local economy.

One of the local business owners, Mr. Tembo, shared his experience of hiring immigrant workers in his construction company. He spoke of the skills and dedication they brought to the job, and how their contributions had helped his business grow. "By embracing the economic potential of immigration, we can build a more prosperous community for all," he declared, his voice filled with conviction.

The villagers nodded in agreement, their eyes shining with determination. They spoke of creating a community where immigrants were welcomed and supported, where their economic contributions were recognized and valued. They acknowledged the role of each individual in harnessing the economic benefits of immigration and pledged to work together to implement the initiatives they had learned.

The local councilors pledged their support, promising to invest in programs that would support immigrant entrepreneurs and workers, laying the foundation for a more prosperous and inclusive future for Kasama. They agreed to work hand in hand with the community, ensuring that every step they took toward economic integration was a step toward a more thriving and united society.

As the sun set, casting a golden glow over the village, Chilufya stood before the gathered multitude. "We have learned that by embracing the economic potential of immigration, we can build a community where everyone prospers," he declared, his voice echoing through the gathering. "Let us embark on this journey together, with vision and determination, knowing that every step we take toward economic integration is a step toward a brighter, more prosperous future."

With unity in their hearts and purpose in their steps, Chilufya and his team set forth, their eyes fixed on the horizon where the promise of prosperity awaited, their resolve unshakeable, their commitment unwavering—the architects of economic growth, the builders of prosperity.

12

Chapter 12: Cultural Policy and Arts Promotion

Cultural Heritage Preservation

"Guardians of Heritage: Cultural Heritage Preservation"

As the morning mist lifted from the rolling hills of Kasama, the ancient baobab tree stood as a testament to the village's rich cultural history. Today, Chilufya and his team gathered to delve into a new chapter of their journey—the importance of cultural policy and arts promotion, starting with the preservation of their cultural heritage. Guided by the "Building Better Communities" handbook, they aimed to understand how to safeguard their traditions while fostering a vibrant, contemporary cultural scene.

Chilufya's voice was filled with reverence as he addressed the assembly. "Our cultural heritage is the soul of our community," he began. "Preserving it is not just about honoring our past but also about inspiring our future."

To gain a deeper understanding of cultural heritage preservation, Chilufya and his team embarked on a journey across Zambia, visiting communities renowned for their dedication to preserving their cultural heritage. Their first destination was the historic town of Livingstonia, known for its preservation of colonial and indigenous cultural sites.

In Livingstonia, they met with Ms. Ngulube, a cultural historian and the curator of the Livingstonia Museum. She passionately explained the importance of preserving cultural artifacts, oral histories, and traditional practices. Chilufya and his team toured the museum, marveling at the carefully preserved relics and listening to stories that spanned generations.

Chilufya and his team were inspired by the meticulous care taken to preserve Livingstonia's cultural heritage. They listened to stories of how the preservation of these artifacts and traditions not only educated visitors but also instilled pride in the local community. The need for a comprehensive cultural heritage preservation strategy became clear, as did the role of education in this endeavor.

Next, the team traveled to the village of Mpika, known for its vibrant traditional music and dance. There, they visited a cultural center where local artists and elders worked together to keep their musical heritage alive. They met with Mr. Mwenya, a renowned traditional musician, who explained how music and dance were integral to their cultural identity.

Mr. Mwenya shared how the cultural center provided a space for young people to learn traditional instruments and dances, ensuring that these art forms were passed down to future generations. He emphasized the importance of community involvement and support in preserving their cultural heritage. Chilufya and his team participated in a traditional dance, experiencing firsthand the joy and unity it brought to the community.

Inspired by Ms. Ngulube's knowledge and Mr. Mwenya's passion, Chilufya and his team returned to Kasama with a renewed sense of purpose. They convened a meeting under the baobab tree, inviting community leaders, residents, and cultural practitioners to join them in discussing strategies for cultural heritage preservation.

Chilufya shared the lessons from Livingstonia and Mpika, illustrating the importance of preserving cultural artifacts, oral histories, and traditional practices. He spoke of the need for educational programs, cultural centers, and community involvement in preserving their heritage.

One of the local elders, Mrs. Kabwe, shared her experience of teaching traditional crafts to the younger generation. She spoke of the pride and connection they felt in learning these skills and the importance of keeping these traditions alive. "By preserving our cultural heritage, we ensure that our history and identity are never lost," she declared, her voice filled with emotion.

The villagers nodded in agreement, their eyes shining with determination. They spoke of creating a community where cultural heritage was cherished and preserved, where every individual felt connected to their roots. They acknowledged the role of each person in safeguarding their traditions and pledged to work together to implement the initiatives they had learned.

The local councilors pledged their support, promising to invest in cultural preservation programs that would lay the foundation for a more vibrant and cohesive future for Kasama. They agreed to work hand in hand with the community, ensuring that every step they took toward preserving their heritage was a step toward a more enriched and united society.

As the sun set, casting a golden glow over the village, Chilufya stood before the gathered multitude. "We have learned that by preserving our cultural heritage, we ensure that our history and identity are never lost," he declared, his voice echoing through the gathering. "Let us embark on this journey together, with respect and dedication, knowing that every step we take toward cultural preservation is a step toward a brighter, more enriched future."

With unity in their hearts and purpose in their steps, Chilufya and his team set forth, their eyes fixed on the horizon where the promise of heritage awaited, their resolve unshakeable, their commitment unwavering—the guardians of heritage, the builders of cultural legacy.

Arts Funding and Support Mechanisms

"Cultivating Creativity: Arts Funding and Support Mechanisms"

As the afternoon sun bathed the village of Kasama in a warm glow, the community gathered once more under the shade of the ancient baobab tree. Today, Chilufya and his team continued their exploration of cultural policy and arts promotion, focusing on the vital aspect of arts funding and support mechanisms. Guided by the "Building Better Communities" handbook, they aimed to cultivate an environment where creativity thrived and artistic expression flourished.

Chilufya's voice rang out with enthusiasm as he addressed the assembly. "The arts are the heartbeat of our community, nourishing our spirits and igniting our imaginations," he proclaimed. "Let us explore how we can provide the support needed for our artists to thrive."

To delve deeper into arts funding and support mechanisms, Chilufya and his team embarked on a journey across Zambia, visiting communities that had successfully nurtured their artistic talents. Their first destination was the bustling city of Lusaka, where they visited an arts council dedicated to supporting local artists.

In Lusaka, they met with Ms. Mwamba, the director of the arts council, who explained the various funding opportunities and support programs available to artists. She spoke of grants, scholarships, and residencies that provided financial assistance and professional development opportunities. Chilufya and his team attended a workshop where artists learned about grant writing and project management, witnessing firsthand the impact of these initiatives.

Chilufya and his team were inspired by the dedication of the arts council to supporting local talent. They listened to stories of artists who had received funding and support, allowing them to pursue their creative endeavors full-time. The need for accessible funding and comprehensive support programs became clear, as did the role of advocacy in promoting the arts.

Next, the team traveled to the town of Kabwe, where they visited a community arts center that provided free workshops and studio space to local artists. There, they met with Mr. Chanda, a sculptor who had benefited from the center's programs.

Mr. Chanda shared how the arts center had provided him with the resources and mentorship needed to develop his craft. He spoke of the sense of community and camaraderie among the artists, and the role of the arts in revitalizing the local economy. Chilufya and his team participated in a pottery workshop, experiencing firsthand the transformative power of artistic expression.

Inspired by Ms. Mwamba's expertise and Mr. Chanda's passion, Chilufya and his team returned to Kasama with a renewed sense of purpose. They convened a meeting under the baobab tree, inviting community leaders, residents, and local artists to join them in discussing strategies for arts funding and support.

Chilufya shared the lessons from Lusaka and Kabwe, illustrating the importance of providing accessible funding and comprehensive support programs for artists. He spoke of the need for grants, workshops, and studio spaces that would empower artists to pursue their passions and contribute to the cultural richness of the community.

One of the local artists, Ms. Sichalwe, shared her experience of struggling to find resources and opportunities to showcase her work. She spoke of the impact that funding and support had on her artistic journey and the importance of investing in the next generation of artists. "By providing the necessary support, we can unlock the full potential of our creative community," she declared, her voice filled with determination.

The villagers nodded in agreement, their eyes shining with excitement. They spoke of creating a community where artists were valued and supported, where their contributions were celebrated and nurtured. They acknowledged the role of each individual in fostering a vibrant arts scene and pledged to work together to implement the initiatives they had learned.

The local councilors pledged their support, promising to invest in arts funding and support programs that would lay the foundation for a more vibrant and culturally rich future for Kasama. They agreed to work hand in hand with the community, ensuring that every step they took toward supporting the arts was a step toward a more creative and inspired society.

As the sun dipped below the horizon, casting a warm glow over the village, Chilufya stood before the gathered multitude. "We have learned that by providing accessible funding and comprehensive support programs, we can unlock the full potential of our creative community," he declared, his voice echoing through the gathering. "Let us embark on this journey together, with passion and dedication, knowing that every step we take toward supporting the arts is a step toward a more vibrant, culturally rich future."

With unity in their hearts and purpose in their steps, Chilufya and his team set forth, their eyes fixed on the horizon where the promise of creativity awaited, their resolve unshakeable, their commitment unwavering—the patrons of the arts, the cultivators of creativity.

Cultural Diversity and Inclusivity

"Harmony in Diversity: Cultural Diversity and Inclusivity"

Underneath the starry night sky, the village of Kasama glowed with a sense of anticipation. Gathered once more beneath the embracing canopy of the ancient baobab tree, Chilufya and his team continued their exploration of cultural policy and arts promotion. Tonight's focus illuminated the essence of their community: embracing cultural diversity and fostering inclusivity. Guided by the "Building Better Communities" handbook, they aimed to create a tapestry where every thread, every shade, contributed to the vibrant mosaic of their shared identity.

Chilufya's voice carried a tone of reverence as he addressed the assembly. "In our diversity lies our strength," he began. "Tonight, let us celebrate the richness of our cultural tapestry and commit to building a community where every voice is heard, and every story is valued."

To delve deeper into the essence of cultural diversity and inclusivity, Chilufya and his team embarked on a journey across Zambia, visiting communities that had embraced their unique blend of cultures. Their first stop was the vibrant town of Livingstone, where they witnessed firsthand the fusion of indigenous traditions and colonial heritage.

In Livingstone, they met with Ms. Chisenga, a cultural ambassador dedicated to bridging divides and fostering understanding among diverse communities. She shared stories of collaboration and coexistence, where people of different backgrounds came together to celebrate their shared humanity. Chilufya and his team participated in cultural festivals, immersing themselves in the sights, sounds, and flavors of Zambia's diverse heritage.

Chilufya and his team were inspired by the spirit of unity that permeated Livingstone's streets. They listened to stories of reconciliation and mutual respect, realizing the transformative power of cultural exchange. The need for inclusive cultural policies and initiatives became clear, as did the role of empathy in fostering understanding.

Next, the team traveled to the bustling city of Kitwe, where they visited a community center that provided a safe space for marginalized groups to express themselves through art and music. There, they met with Mr. Mulenga, a community organizer who believed in the power of creativity to transcend barriers.

Mr. Mulenga shared stories of how the community center had become a beacon of hope for refugees, migrants, and people with disabilities, providing them with opportunities to showcase their talents and tell their stories. Chilufya and his team attended performances and exhibitions, witnessing the transformative impact of art in fostering empathy and understanding.

Inspired by Ms. Chisenga's vision and Mr. Mulenga's dedication, Chilufya and his team returned to Kasama with a renewed sense of purpose. They convened a meeting under the baobab tree, inviting community leaders, residents, and representatives from diverse cultural groups to join them in discussing strategies for promoting cultural diversity and inclusivity.

Chilufya shared the lessons from Livingstone and Kitwe, illustrating the importance of embracing cultural diversity and fostering inclusivity in their community. He spoke of the need for inclusive cultural events, educational programs, and policies that would celebrate the unique contributions of every individual.

One of the local elders, Mr. Bwalya, shared his experience of growing up in a community where people of different backgrounds lived side by side in harmony. He spoke of the richness that diversity brought to their lives and the importance of passing down this legacy to future generations.

"By embracing our diversity and fostering inclusivity, we can build a community where every individual feels valued and respected," he declared, his voice filled with conviction.

The villagers nodded in agreement, their hearts filled with a sense of pride and belonging. They spoke of creating a community where cultural diversity was celebrated and differences were embraced, where every individual felt a sense of belonging and connection. They acknowledged the role of each person in fostering understanding and pledged to work together to implement the initiatives they had learned.

The local councilors pledged their support, promising to invest in inclusive cultural events and programs that would celebrate the diversity of their community. They agreed to work hand in hand with the community, ensuring that every step they took toward promoting cultural diversity and inclusivity was a step toward a more harmonious and united society.

As the stars twinkled overhead, casting a soft glow over the village, Chilufya stood before the gathered multitude. "We have learned that in our diversity lies our strength," he declared, his voice echoing through the gathering. "Let us embark on this journey together, with open hearts and minds, knowing that every step we take toward embracing cultural diversity and fostering inclusivity is a step toward a brighter, more harmonious future."

With unity in their hearts and purpose in their steps, Chilufya and his team set forth, their eyes fixed on the horizon where the promise of unity awaited, their resolve unshakeable, their commitment unwavering—the champions of diversity, the architects of inclusivity.

Public Spaces for Arts and Cultural Expression

"Spaces of Expression: Fostering Art and Culture in Public Spaces"

Under the gentle moonlight, the village of Kasama buzzed with anticipation. Once again, beneath the sprawling branches of the ancient baobab tree, Chilufya and his team delved deeper into their exploration of cultural policy and arts promotion. Tonight's focus illuminated the importance of public spaces as platforms for artistic and cultural expression. Guided by the "Building Better Communities" handbook, they aimed to cultivate environments where creativity flourished and cultural exchange thrived.

Chilufya's voice resonated with passion as he addressed the assembly. "Our public spaces are more than just places; they are stages where our stories unfold, and our culture comes to life," he proclaimed. "Let us explore how we can transform our community spaces into vibrant hubs of artistic and cultural expression."

To further explore the role of public spaces in fostering art and culture, Chilufya and his team embarked on a journey across Zambia, visiting communities where public spaces served as dynamic platforms for creative expression. Their first stop was the bustling city of Ndola, where they witnessed the transformation of a vacant lot into a vibrant community arts park.

In Ndola, they met with Mr. Mwale, the visionary behind the arts park project. He shared stories of how the once-neglected space had been revitalized through collaborative efforts, becoming a hub for artists, performers, and community members alike. Chilufya and his team marveled at the colorful murals adorning the walls and the lively performances that filled the air.

Chilufya and his team were inspired by the power of public spaces to bring people together and spark creativity. They listened to stories of how the arts park had become a symbol of community pride and a catalyst for social cohesion. The need for accessible and inclusive public spaces for artistic and cultural expression became clear, as did the role of community engagement in their creation.

Next, the team traveled to the historic town of Livingstone, where they visited a public square that served as a gathering place for cultural events and performances. There, they met with Ms. Banda, a community organizer who had spearheaded efforts to revitalize the square.

Ms. Banda shared stories of how the square had become a focal point for celebrations, festivals, and cultural exchanges, fostering a sense of belonging and connection among residents and visitors alike. Chilufya and his team participated in a traditional dance performance, feeling the energy and vibrancy of the square come alive.

Inspired by Mr. Mwale's vision and Ms. Banda's dedication, Chilufya and his team returned to Kasama with a renewed sense of purpose. They convened a meeting under the baobab tree, inviting community leaders, residents, and artists to join them in discussing strategies for transforming public spaces into vibrant hubs of artistic and cultural expression.

Chilufya shared the lessons from Ndola and Livingstone, illustrating the importance of creating inclusive and accessible public spaces that celebrate the diversity of their community. He spoke of the need for collaborative efforts, creative programming, and community engagement in reimagining their public spaces as platforms for artistic and cultural exchange.

One of the local artists, Ms. Tembo, shared her vision for transforming the village square into a vibrant arts and cultural hub. She spoke of hosting art exhibitions, live performances, and cultural workshops that would bring people together and celebrate their shared heritage. "By transforming our public spaces, we can create opportunities for connection, collaboration, and creativity," she declared, her voice filled with excitement.

The villagers nodded in agreement, their hearts filled with a sense of possibility. They spoke of reclaiming their public spaces as places of joy and inspiration, where creativity flourished, and culture thrived. They acknowledged the role of each person in shaping the future of their community and pledged to work together to implement the initiatives they had learned.

The local councilors pledged their support, promising to invest in the revitalization of public spaces that would serve as catalysts for artistic and cultural expression. They agreed to work hand in hand with the community, ensuring that every step they took toward transforming their public spaces was a step toward a more vibrant, connected, and culturally rich society.

As the moon cast its gentle glow over the village, Chilufya stood before the gathered multitude. "We have learned that our public spaces are more than just places; they are stages where our stories unfold, and our culture comes to life," he declared, his voice echoing through the gathering. "Let us embark on this journey together, with imagination and determination, knowing that every step we take toward transforming our public spaces is a step toward a brighter, more vibrant future."

With unity in their hearts and purpose in their steps, Chilufya and his team set forth, their eyes fixed on the horizon where the promise of creativity awaited, their resolve unshakeable, their commitment unwavering—the stewards of public spaces, the champions of artistic expression.

Creative Economy Development

"The Creative Canvas: Nurturing a Thriving Creative Economy"

Underneath the blanket of stars, the village of Kasama hummed with anticipation. Once again, gathered beneath the protective embrace of the ancient baobab tree, Chilufya and his team delved deeper into their exploration of cultural policy and arts promotion. Tonight's focus illuminated the transformative power of nurturing a vibrant creative economy. Guided by the "Building Better Communities" handbook, they aimed to cultivate an environment where creativity was not only celebrated but also served as an engine for economic growth and community development.

Chilufya's voice echoed with enthusiasm as he addressed the assembly. "In the tapestry of our community, creativity is the thread that weaves opportunity and prosperity," he proclaimed. "Let us explore how we can harness the power of our creative talents to build a thriving economy and a brighter future for all."

To further explore the potential of nurturing a creative economy, Chilufya and his team embarked on a journey across

Zambia, visiting communities where the arts served as catalysts for economic growth. Their first stop was the bustling city of Lusaka, where they witnessed the transformation of abandoned warehouses into vibrant creative hubs.

In Lusaka, they met with Mr. Sibanda, a visionary entrepreneur who had founded a creative collective that provided workspace and support services to local artists and designers. He shared stories of how the collective had revitalized the neighborhood, attracting visitors and investors alike. Chilufya and his team marveled at the innovative products and designs being produced in the collective's studios.

Chilufya and his team were inspired by the potential of the creative economy to revitalize communities and create opportunities for employment and entrepreneurship. They listened to stories of how the collective had provided a platform for local talent to thrive and how it had become a hub for collaboration and innovation. The need for strategic investment and supportive policies to nurture the creative economy became clear, as did the role of partnerships in its development.

Next, the team traveled to the town of Kabwe, where they visited a community arts market that showcased the work of local artisans and craftsmen. There, they met with Ms. Mulenga, a jewelry designer who had turned her passion into a successful business.

Ms. Mulenga shared stories of how the arts market had provided her with a platform to showcase her designs and connect with customers. She spoke of the economic opportunities that had been created for artisans and the positive impact it had on the local economy. Chilufya and his team browsed through the colorful stalls, marveling at the diversity of talent on display.

Inspired by Mr. Sibanda's vision and Ms. Mulenga's entrepreneurship, Chilufya and his team returned to Kasama with a renewed sense of purpose. They convened a meeting under the baobab tree, inviting community leaders, residents, and creative entrepreneurs to join them in discussing strategies for nurturing a thriving creative economy.

Chilufya shared the lessons from Lusaka and Kabwe, illustrating the importance of investing in creative infrastructure and supporting local talent. He spoke of the need for incubator programs, business training, and access to markets that would empower creative entrepreneurs to succeed. He emphasized the role of collaboration and networking in building a resilient creative ecosystem.

One of the local artisans, Mr. Mwape, shared his experience of starting a pottery business with support from a local incubator program. He spoke of the challenges he faced and the opportunities that arose from connecting with other entrepreneurs and accessing new markets. "By investing in the creative economy, we can unlock the potential of our community and create a better future for generations to come," he declared, his voice filled with determination.

The villagers nodded in agreement, their minds buzzing with ideas and possibilities. They spoke of creating a community where creativity was valued and supported, where artists and entrepreneurs could thrive and contribute to the local economy. They acknowledged the role of each person in shaping the future of their community and pledged to work together to implement the initiatives they had learned.

The local councilors pledged their support, promising to

invest in creative infrastructure and develop policies that would foster a thriving creative economy. They agreed to work hand in hand with the community, ensuring that every step they took toward nurturing the creative economy was a step toward a more prosperous and vibrant society.

As the stars twinkled overhead, casting a soft glow over the village, Chilufya stood before the gathered multitude. "We have learned that in the tapestry of our community, creativity is the thread that weaves opportunity and prosperity," he declared, his voice echoing through the gathering. "Let us embark on this journey together, with vision and determination, knowing that every step we take toward nurturing the creative economy is a step toward a brighter, more vibrant future."

With unity in their hearts and purpose in their steps, Chilufya and his team set forth, their eyes fixed on the horizon where the promise of creativity awaited, their resolve unshakeable, their commitment unwavering—the architects of opportunity, the champions of innovation.

International Cultural Exchange Programs

"Bridging Cultures: International Cultural Exchange Programs"

Under the twinkling stars, the village of Kasama buzzed with anticipation. Once more, gathered beneath the protective canopy of the ancient baobab tree, Chilufya and his team delved deeper into their exploration of cultural policy and arts promotion. Tonight's focus illuminated the transformative power of international cultural exchange programs. Guided by the "Building Better Communities" handbook, they aimed to create bridges of understanding and cooperation that transcended borders and celebrated diversity.

Chilufya's voice carried a note of excitement as he addressed the assembly. "In the tapestry of humanity, every thread, every hue, contributes to the richness of our shared story," he declared. "Tonight, let us explore how we can weave connections with distant lands, fostering understanding and appreciation of our global cultural heritage."

To delve deeper into the potential of international cultural exchange programs, Chilufya and his team embarked on a journey across Zambia, visiting communities that had embraced the transformative power of cross-cultural dialogue. Their first destination was the capital city of Lusaka, where they witnessed the impact of a cultural exchange program with a sister city abroad.

In Lusaka, they met with Ms. Ngoma, a cultural liaison who had facilitated exchanges between local artists and their counterparts in a sister city overseas. She shared stories of how these exchanges had broadened perspectives, inspired creativity, and forged lasting friendships across continents. Chilufya and his team marveled at the artworks and performances that bore the imprint of cross-cultural collaboration.

Chilufya and his team were inspired by the potential of international cultural exchange programs to foster mutual understanding and appreciation. They listened to stories of how these programs had transcended language and cultural barriers, creating bonds of friendship and solidarity. The need for continued investment and support for such initiatives became clear, as did the role of cultural diplomacy in promoting peace and cooperation.

Next, the team traveled to the picturesque town of Living-stone, where they visited a cultural center that hosted artists and scholars from around the world. There, they met with Mr. Chanda, a curator who had organized exhibitions and workshops that showcased the diversity of global culture.

Mr. Chanda shared stories of how the cultural center had become a melting pot of ideas and perspectives, fostering dialogue and mutual respect among participants. He spoke of the transformative impact of cultural exchange on both visitors and hosts, enriching lives and expanding horizons. Chilufya and his team participated in a traditional music performance, feeling the universal language of music connect hearts across continents.

Inspired by Ms. Ngoma's dedication and Mr. Chanda's vision, Chilufya and his team returned to Kasama with a renewed sense of purpose. They convened a meeting under the baobab tree, inviting community leaders, residents, and cultural enthusiasts to join them in discussing strategies for fostering international cultural exchange.

Chilufya shared the lessons from Lusaka and Livingstone, illustrating the importance of building bridges of under-standing and cooperation with distant lands. He spoke of the need for partnerships and collaborations that would facilitate cultural exchange and promote global citizenship. He emphasized the role of cultural diplomacy in building a more peaceful and interconnected world.

One of the local artists, Ms. Tembo, shared her experience of participating in an international residency program. She spoke of the transformative impact of living and working in a foreign country, gaining new perspectives and forging lifelong friendships. "By opening our hearts and minds to the world, we can create a more inclusive and compassionate community," she declared, her voice filled with conviction.

The villagers nodded in agreement, their hearts filled with a sense of possibility. They spoke of embracing diversity and celebrating the richness of global culture, knowing that every interaction, every exchange, was a step toward a more interconnected world. They acknowledged the role of each person in building bridges of understanding and pledged to work together to implement the initiatives they had learned.

The local councilors pledged their support, promising to invest in international cultural exchange programs that would enrich the lives of their community members and promote cross-cultural understanding. They agreed to work hand in hand with the community, ensuring that every step they took toward fostering international cultural exchange was a step toward a more peaceful, inclusive, and interconnected society.

As the stars shimmered overhead, casting a soft glow over the village, Chilufya stood before the gathered multitude. "We have learned that in the tapestry of humanity, every thread, every hue, contributes to the richness of our shared story," he declared, his voice resonating with hope and optimism. "Let us embark on this journey together, with open hearts and minds, knowing that every step we take toward fostering international cultural exchange is a step toward a brighter, more harmonious future."

With unity in their hearts and purpose in their steps, Chilufya and his team set forth, their eyes fixed on the horizon where the promise of global solidarity awaited, their resolve unshakeable, their commitment unwavering—the ambassadors of culture, the architects of understanding.

13

Chapter 13: Technology Policy and Digital Governance

Internet Governance and Digital Rights

"Navigating the Digital Frontier: Internet Governance and Digital Rights"

Beneath the canopy of stars, the village of Kasama hummed with anticipation. Once more, gathered beneath the ancient baobab tree, Chilufya and his team embarked on a new chapter of exploration: technology policy and digital governance. Tonight's focus illuminated the intricate landscape of internet governance and the imperative of safeguarding digital rights. Guided by the "Building Better Communities" handbook, they aimed to navigate the digital frontier with wisdom and foresight.

Chilufya's voice reverberated with determination as he addressed the assembly. "In the vast expanse of the digital realm, we must chart a course guided by principles of equity, transparency, and respect for human rights," he proclaimed. "Tonight, let us embark on a journey to understand the complexities of internet governance and safeguard the digital rights of our community."

To delve deeper into the realm of internet governance and digital rights, Chilufya and his team embarked on a virtual journey, exploring the digital landscape and engaging with experts from around the world. Their first stop was a virtual conference on digital governance, where they connected with policymakers, technologists, and activists.

In the virtual conference, they met with Ms. Kamanga, a digital rights advocate who had been instrumental in shaping national policies to protect online freedoms. She shared stories of the challenges posed by emerging technologies and the importance of establishing frameworks that upheld human rights in the digital age. Chilufya and his team listened intently, realizing the need for informed decision-making and collaboration in addressing digital governance issues.

Chilufya and his team were inspired by the passion and dedication of digital rights advocates like Ms. Kamanga. They learned about the principles of internet governance, such as openness, accessibility, and accountability, and the importance of protecting online freedoms, privacy, and data sovereignty. The need for community engagement and grassroots advocacy in shaping technology policy became clear, as did the role of education in promoting digital literacy and awareness.

Next, the team explored innovative approaches to digital governance in the bustling city of Lusaka, where they met with Mr. Musonda, a technology entrepreneur who had developed a mobile app to promote civic engagement and transparency.

He shared stories of how the app had empowered citizens to report issues, access government services, and participate in decision-making processes.

Mr. Musonda's innovative solution demonstrated the transformative potential of technology in enhancing governance and promoting civic participation. Chilufya and his team marveled at the power of digital tools to bridge divides and empower communities, realizing the importance of harnessing technology for the public good.

Inspired by Ms. Kamanga's advocacy and Mr. Musonda's innovation, Chilufya and his team returned to Kasama with a renewed sense of purpose. They convened a meeting under the baobab tree, inviting community leaders, residents, and technology enthusiasts to join them in discussing strategies for navigating the digital frontier.

Chilufya shared the lessons from the virtual conference and their visit to Lusaka, illustrating the importance of upholding digital rights and harnessing technology for the public good. He spoke of the need for transparent and accountable governance structures that safeguarded online freedoms and protected users' privacy and data. He emphasized the role of community engagement in shaping technology policy and promoting digital literacy.

One of the local activists, Ms. Mulenga, shared her experience of advocating for digital rights in the community. She spoke of the challenges posed by online censorship, surveillance, and misinformation and the importance of raising awareness and mobilizing support for digital rights advocacy. "By standing together and speaking out, we can ensure that the digital future is one of freedom, equality, and justice," she declared, her voice filled with determination.

The villagers nodded in agreement, their minds buzzing with ideas and possibilities. They spoke of creating a community where technology served as a tool for empowerment and inclusion, where digital rights were respected, and online freedoms protected. They acknowledged the role of each person in shaping the digital future of their community and pledged to work together to implement the initiatives they had learned.

The local councilors pledged their support, promising to prioritize technology policy and digital governance issues in their decision-making. They agreed to work hand in hand with the community, ensuring that every step they took toward navigating the digital frontier was a step toward a more equitable, inclusive, and rights-respecting society.

As the stars shimmered overhead, casting a soft glow over the village, Chilufya stood before the gathered multitude. "We have learned that in the vast expanse of the digital realm, we must chart a course guided by principles of equity, transparency, and respect for human rights," he declared, his voice resonating with hope and determination. "Let us embark on this journey together, with wisdom and foresight, knowing that every step we take toward safeguarding digital rights is a step toward a brighter, more just future."

With unity in their hearts and purpose in their steps, Chilufya and his team set forth, their eyes fixed on the horizon where the promise of a digital society awaited, their resolve unshakeable, their commitment unwavering—the guardians of digital rights, the architects of a digital future.

Data Privacy and Cybersecurity Policies

"Guardians of the Digital Realm: Protecting Data Privacy and Cybersecurity"

Under the tranquil night sky, the village of Kasama pulsed with anticipation. Gathered once more beneath the protective branches of the ancient baobab tree, Chilufya and his team delved into the next chapter of their exploration: technology policy and digital governance. Tonight's focus illuminated the critical importance of safeguarding data privacy and cybersecurity in the digital age. Guided by the "Building Better Communities" handbook, they aimed to become guardians of the digital realm, ensuring the protection of their community's digital assets.

Chilufya's voice echoed with urgency as he addressed the assembly. "In the vast expanse of the digital realm, our most valuable assets are not gold or jewels, but the data that flows through our networks," he proclaimed. "Tonight, let us explore how we can fortify our defenses and protect the privacy and security of our community's digital footprint."

To delve deeper into the realm of data privacy and cybersecurity, Chilufya and his team embarked on a journey across Zambia, visiting communities that had implemented innovative approaches to safeguarding their digital assets. Their first destination was the bustling city of Kitwe, where they met with Mr. Tembo, a cybersecurity expert who had developed a comprehensive cybersecurity framework for local businesses.

In Kitwe, they witnessed firsthand the devastating impact of cyberattacks on small businesses and individuals. Mr. Tembo shared stories of data breaches, ransomware attacks, and identity theft, highlighting the need for robust cybersecurity measures to protect against evolving threats. Chilufya and his team listened intently, realizing the importance of proactive measures to mitigate risks and strengthen defenses.

Chilufya and his team were inspired by Mr. Tembo's dedication to cybersecurity awareness and education. They learned about the principles of data privacy and the importance of implementing policies and protocols to safeguard sensitive information. The need for collaboration and information sharing in the fight against cyber threats became clear, as did the role of community resilience in building a cyber-secure society.

Next, the team explored innovative approaches to data privacy in the capital city of Lusaka, where they met with Ms. Banda, a data protection officer who had developed a data privacy framework for government agencies. She shared stories of how the framework had enhanced transparency, accountability, and trust in the government's handling of personal data.

Ms. Banda's work demonstrated the transformative potential of data privacy policies in building public trust and confidence in digital services. Chilufya and his team marveled at the intricacies of data protection laws and regulations, realizing the importance of empowering individuals to exercise control over their personal information.

Inspired by Mr. Tembo's expertise and Ms. Banda's leadership, Chilufya and his team returned to Kasama with a renewed sense of purpose. They convened a meeting under the baobab tree, inviting community leaders, residents, and technology experts to join them in discussing strategies for protecting data privacy and cybersecurity.

Chilufya shared the lessons from Kitwe and Lusaka, illustrating the importance of implementing robust cybersecurity measures and data privacy policies. He spoke of the need for awareness and education to empower individuals to protect themselves online and the importance of collaboration and partnerships in addressing cyber threats.

One of the local entrepreneurs, Mr. Mwansa, shared his experience of falling victim to a cyberattack and the devastating impact it had on his business. He spoke of the importance of investing in cybersecurity measures and adopting best practices to prevent future attacks. "By prioritizing cybersecurity and data privacy, we can safeguard our community's digital future and protect the integrity of our data," he declared, his voice filled with determination.

The villagers nodded in agreement, their minds focused on the task ahead. They spoke of creating a community where data privacy and cybersecurity were paramount, where individuals felt safe and secure in their online interactions. They acknowledged the role of each person in safeguarding the digital realm and pledged to work together to implement the initiatives they had learned.

The local councilors pledged their support, promising to prioritize data privacy and cybersecurity issues in their policymaking. They agreed to work hand in hand with the community, ensuring that every step they took toward protecting data privacy and cybersecurity was a step toward a more resilient, secure, and digitally empowered society.

As the stars cast their gentle glow over the village, Chilufya stood before the gathered multitude. "We have learned that in the vast expanse of the digital realm, our most valuable assets are not gold or jewels, but the data that flows through our networks," he declared, his voice resolute. "Let us embark on this journey together, with vigilance and determination, knowing that every step we take toward protecting data privacy and cybersecurity is a step toward a safer, more secure digital future."

With unity in their hearts and purpose in their steps, Chilufya and his team set forth, their eyes fixed on the horizon where the promise of a secure digital realm awaited, their resolve unshakeable, their commitment unwavering—the guardians of data privacy, the sentinels of cybersecurity.

Regulation of Emerging Technologies

"Embracing Innovation: Regulating Emerging Technologies"

Under the tranquil night sky, the village of Kasama gathered once more beneath the sprawling branches of the ancient baobab tree. Chilufya and his team delved further into their exploration of technology policy and digital governance. Tonight's focus illuminated the delicate balance between fostering innovation and regulating emerging technologies. Guided by the "Building Better Communities" handbook, they aimed to navigate the evolving landscape of technological advancement with wisdom and foresight.

Chilufya's voice carried a tone of contemplation as he addressed the assembly. "In the ever-changing landscape of technological innovation, we must tread cautiously, ensuring that progress is accompanied by responsibility and account-ability," he proclaimed. "Tonight, let us explore how we can embrace innovation while safeguarding the well-being of our community."

To delve deeper into the realm of regulating emerging technologies, Chilufya and his team embarked on a journey across Zambia, visiting communities that had grappled with the challenges and opportunities presented by cutting-edge innovations. Their first destination was the vibrant city of Ndola, where they met with Dr. Banda, a renowned expert in artificial intelligence (AI) ethics and regulation.

In Ndola, they witnessed the transformative potential of AI technologies in healthcare, agriculture, and education. Dr. Banda shared stories of how AI-powered systems had improved efficiency, productivity, and quality of life for citizens. Yet, he also cautioned against the risks of unchecked AI deployment, emphasizing the need for ethical guidelines and regulatory frameworks.

Chilufya and his team were inspired by Dr. Banda's insights into the ethical implications of AI technologies. They learned about the principles of responsible AI development, such as transparency, fairness, and accountability, and the importance of ensuring that AI systems were aligned with human values and rights. The need for interdisciplinary collaboration and public engagement in shaping AI policies became clear, as did the role of governance in mitigating risks and maximizing benefits.

Next, the team explored the regulation of biotechnology in the agricultural heartland of Chipata, where they met with Dr. Mulenga, a biotechnologist who had been involved in the development of genetically modified (GM) crops. She shared stories of how GM technologies had increased crop yields, reduced pesticide use, and improved food security for smallholder farmers.

Dr. Mulenga's work highlighted the potential of biotechnology to address pressing agricultural challenges, yet it also raised concerns about environmental impact and food safety. Chilufya and his team grappled with the complexities of regulating emerging biotechnologies, realizing the need for evidence-based decision-making and stakeholder engagement in policymaking processes.

Inspired by Dr. Banda's expertise and Dr. Mulenga's insights, Chilufya and his team returned to Kasama with a renewed sense of purpose. They convened a meeting under the baobab tree, inviting community leaders, residents, and technology experts to join them in discussing strategies for regulating emerging technologies.

Chilufya shared the lessons from Ndola and Chipata, illustrating the importance of balancing innovation with responsibility in the adoption of emerging technologies. He spoke of the need for regulatory frameworks that fostered innovation while safeguarding public health, safety, and welfare. He emphasized the role of community input and democratic governance in shaping technology policies that reflected the values and aspirations of society.

One of the local farmers, Mr. Kabwe, shared his perspective on the potential benefits and risks of adopting biotechnologies in agriculture. He spoke of the need for transparent and science-based regulation to ensure that new technologies were safe, sustainable, and equitable. "By harnessing the power of innovation responsibly, we can create a better future for our community and the generations to come," he declared, his voice filled with conviction.

The villagers nodded in agreement, their minds buzzing with ideas and possibilities. They spoke of creating a community where technological innovation was embraced as a force for good, where the benefits of progress were shared equitably, and the risks were mitigated responsibly. They acknowledged the role of each person in shaping the technological future of their community and pledged to work together to implement the initiatives they had learned.

The local councilors pledged their support, promising to prioritize the regulation of emerging technologies in their policymaking. They agreed to work hand in hand with the community, ensuring that every step they took toward embracing innovation was a step toward a safer, more sustainable, and more prosperous future.

As the stars cast their gentle glow over the village, Chilufya stood before the gathered multitude. "We have learned that in the ever-changing landscape of technological innovation, we must tread cautiously, ensuring that progress is accompanied by responsibility and accountability," he declared, his voice resolute. "Let us embark on this journey together, with wisdom and foresight, knowing that every step we take toward regulating emerging technologies is a step toward a brighter, more sustainable future."

With unity in their hearts and purpose in their steps, Chilufya and his team set forth, their eyes fixed on the horizon where the promise of technological advancement awaited, their resolve unshakeable, their commitment unwavering— the stewards of innovation, the guardians of progress.

E-Government and Digital Service Delivery

"Empowering Communities: E-Government and Digital Service Delivery"

Under the canopy of twinkling stars, the village of Kasama buzzed with anticipation. Once again gathered beneath the ancient baobab tree, Chilufya and his team delved deeper into their exploration of technology policy and digital governance. Tonight's focus illuminated the transformative potential of e-government and digital service delivery. Guided by the "Building Better Communities" handbook, they aimed to empower their community through the efficient and accessible delivery of public services.

Chilufya's voice resonated with purpose as he addressed the assembly. "In the digital age, governance must evolve to meet the needs of our ever-connected society," he proclaimed. "Tonight, let us explore how e-government and digital service delivery can empower our community and enhance the quality of life for all."

To delve deeper into the realm of e-government and digital service delivery, Chilufya and his team embarked on a journey across Zambia, visiting communities that had embraced digital technologies to streamline public services. Their first destination was the bustling city of Lusaka, where they met with Mrs. Mwansa, a government official leading the implementation of an e-government platform.

In Lusaka, they witnessed firsthand the efficiency and transparency brought about by the e-government platform. Mrs. Mwansa shared stories of how citizens could now access government services online, from applying for permits to paying taxes, saving time and reducing bureaucracy. Chilufya and his team marveled at the power of digitalization to enhance citizen engagement and improve governance outcomes.

Chilufya and his team were inspired by Mrs. Mwansa's vision for a more responsive and citizen-centric government. They learned about the principles of e-government, such as accessibility, inclusivity, and interoperability, and the importance of leveraging digital technologies to deliver services more effectively and efficiently. The need for capacity building and digital literacy initiatives to ensure that all citizens could benefit from e-government services became clear, as did the role of partnerships and collaboration in driving digital transformation.

Next, the team explored innovative approaches to digital service delivery in the remote town of Mongu, where they met with Mr. Wamundila, a community leader spearheading a mobile-based healthcare initiative. He shared stories of how mobile health clinics and telemedicine services had improved access to healthcare for underserved populations, reducing disparities and saving lives.

Mr. Wamundila's work highlighted the potential of digital technologies to address pressing social challenges and improve the well-being of communities. Chilufya and his team recognized the importance of tailoring digital solutions to local contexts and ensuring that technology served the needs of the most vulnerable members of society.

Inspired by Mrs. Mwansa's leadership and Mr. Wamundila's innovation, Chilufya and his team returned to Kasama with a renewed sense of purpose. They convened a meeting under the baobab tree, inviting community leaders, residents, and technology experts to join them in discussing strategies for harnessing e-government and digital service delivery.

Chilufya shared the lessons from Lusaka and Mongu, illustrating the potential of digital technologies to enhance governance and improve service delivery. He spoke of the need for user-centered design and inclusive approaches to ensure that e-government services met the diverse needs of the community. He emphasized the role of community engagement in shaping digital transformation initiatives and promoting digital inclusion.

One of the local teachers, Mrs. Chanda, shared her experience of using digital tools to enhance education delivery in remote areas. She spoke of the opportunities presented by e-learning platforms and digital textbooks to expand access to quality education and empower learners to reach their full potential. "By harnessing the power of technology, we can bridge the digital divide and create a more equitable and inclusive society," she declared, her voice filled with optimism.

The villagers nodded in agreement, their hearts filled with hope and determination. They spoke of creating a community where e-government services were accessible to all, where technology was used to improve the lives of every citizen. They acknowledged the role of each person in driving digital transformation and pledged to work together to implement the initiatives they had learned.

The local councilors pledged their support, promising to prioritize e-government and digital service delivery in their policymaking. They agreed to work hand in hand with the community, ensuring that every step they took toward harnessing digital technologies was a step toward a more responsive, efficient, and citizen-centric government.

As the stars cast their gentle glow over the village, Chilufya stood before the gathered multitude. "We have learned that in the digital age, governance must evolve to meet the needs of our ever-connected society," he declared, his voice echoing with conviction. "Let us embark on this journey together, with innovation and inclusivity, knowing that every step we take toward e-government and digital service delivery is a step toward a brighter, more empowered future."

With unity in their hearts and purpose in their steps, Chilufya and his team set forth, their eyes fixed on the horizon where the promise of digital empowerment awaited, their resolve unshakeable, their commitment unwavering— the architects of e-government, the champions of digital inclusion.

Access to Information and Digital Inclusion

"Bridging the Digital Divide: Access to Information and Digital Inclusion"

Beneath the vast expanse of the night sky, the village of Kasama hummed with anticipation. Once more gathered beneath the ancient baobab tree, Chilufya and his team continued their exploration of technology policy and digital governance. Tonight's focus illuminated the crucial importance of ensuring access to information and promoting digital inclusion. Guided by the "Building Better Communities" handbook, they aimed to bridge the digital divide and empower every member of their community with the tools for success.

Chilufya's voice carried a tone of determination as he addressed the assembly. "In the digital era, access to information is the key to unlocking opportunity and empowering individuals," he proclaimed. "Tonight, let us explore how we can bridge the digital divide and ensure that every member of our community has the tools they need to thrive."

To delve deeper into the realm of access to information and digital inclusion, Chilufya and his team embarked on a journey across Zambia, visiting communities that had pioneered initiatives to promote digital literacy and connectivity. Their first stop was the bustling town of Kabwe, where they met with Mr. Phiri, a local entrepreneur who had established a community library equipped with computers and internet access.

In Kabwe, they witnessed firsthand the transformative impact of access to information on education, entrepreneurship, and civic engagement. Mr. Phiri shared stories of how the community library had become a hub for learning and innovation, empowering individuals of all ages to acquire new skills and pursue their dreams. Chilufya and his team marveled at the power of digital connectivity to break down barriers and expand opportunities.

Chilufya and his team were inspired by Mr. Phiri's commitment to digital inclusion. They learned about the importance of providing affordable internet access and digital literacy training to underserved communities, and the role of public-private partnerships in closing the digital divide. The need for targeted interventions to address barriers such as language, literacy, and disability became clear, as did the importance of community engagement in shaping digital inclusion strategies.

Next, the team explored innovative approaches to promoting digital literacy in the rural village of Chongwe, where they met with Ms. Mulenga, a local teacher who had established a digital skills training program for women and girls. She shared stories of how the program had empowered participants to harness the power of technology to improve their lives and communities.

Ms. Mulenga's work highlighted the transformative potential of digital literacy in promoting gender equality and social inclusion. Chilufya and his team recognized the importance of addressing systemic barriers to digital access and participation, and the need for holistic approaches that empowered individuals to fully participate in the digital economy.

Inspired by Mr. Phiri's vision and Ms. Mulenga's dedication, Chilufya and his team returned to Kasama with a renewed sense of purpose. They convened a meeting under the baobab tree, inviting community leaders, residents, and technology experts to join them in discussing strategies for promoting digital inclusion.

Chilufya shared the lessons from Kabwe and Chongwe, illustrating the importance of ensuring that no one was left behind in the digital age. He spoke of the need for policies and programs that addressed the unique needs and challenges of underserved communities, and the importance of empowering individuals to harness the full potential of digital technologies. He emphasized the role of community-led initiatives in driving digital inclusion and promoting social cohesion.

One of the local elders, Mr. Kunda, shared his perspective on the transformative impact of access to information on community development. He spoke of the opportunities presented by digital connectivity to preserve cultural heritage, promote economic growth, and enhance democratic participation. "By bridging the digital divide, we can create a more inclusive and equitable society where every member has the opportunity to thrive," he declared, his voice filled with conviction.

The villagers nodded in agreement, their hearts stirred by the possibilities of a more connected and inclusive future. They spoke of creating a community where digital literacy was a fundamental right, where technology was a tool for empowerment and social change. They acknowledged the role of each person in breaking down barriers and building bridges to opportunity, and pledged to work together to implement the initiatives they had learned.

The local councilors pledged their support, promising to prioritize digital inclusion in their policymaking and resource allocation. They agreed to work hand in hand with the community, ensuring that every step they took toward bridging the digital divide was a step toward a more equitable, inclusive, and prosperous future.

As the stars cast their gentle glow over the village, Chilufya stood before the gathered multitude. "We have learned that in the digital era, access to information is the key to unlocking opportunity and empowering individuals," he declared, his voice resonating with hope and determination. "Let us embark on this journey together, with empathy and determination, knowing that every step we take toward digital inclusion is a step toward a brighter, more inclusive future."

With unity in their hearts and purpose in their steps, Chilufya and his team set forth, their eyes fixed on the horizon where the promise of digital empowerment awaited, their resolve unshakeable, their commitment unwavering—the champions of access, the architects of inclusion.

Ethical Use of Technology in Governance

"Navigating the Ethical Horizon: Technology's Role in Governance"

Underneath the sprawling branches of the age-old baobab tree, the village of Kasama had gathered once more. With a sense of reverence, Chilufya and his team continued their expedition through technology policy and digital governance. Tonight's focus unveiled the intricate balance between technological advancement and ethical governance. Guided by the "Building Better Communities" handbook, they aimed to navigate the ethical horizon, ensuring that technology served as a tool for progress while upholding the values of integrity and responsibility.

Chilufya's voice resonated with solemnity as he addressed the assembly. "In the realm of governance, technology holds immense power, but with power comes responsibility," he declared. "Tonight, let us explore how we can harness technology ethically to serve our community and uphold the principles of justice and accountability."

To delve deeper into the ethical landscape of technology in governance, Chilufya and his team embarked on a journey across Zambia, visiting communities that grappled with the complexities of technological ethics. Their first destination was the capital city of Lusaka, where they met with Dr. Ngoma, an expert in digital ethics and governance.

In Lusaka, they witnessed the transformative potential of technology in improving governance outcomes, from enhancing transparency to increasing civic engagement. Dr. Ngoma shared stories of how digital tools had revolutionized public participation and decision-making processes, empowering citizens to hold their government accountable. Chilufya and his team marveled at the power of technology to foster a culture of openness and accountability in governance.

Chilufya and his team were inspired by Dr. Ngoma's insights into the ethical dimensions of technology in governance. They learned about the importance of data privacy, algorithmic transparency, and digital rights in ensuring that technology served the public good. The need for robust ethical frameworks and oversight mechanisms to mitigate the risks of technology misuse became clear, as did the role of citizen engagement in shaping ethical governance practices.

Next, the team explored innovative approaches to digital ethics in the rural town of Mongu, where they met with Mr. Sibanda, a community leader advocating for the ethical use of drones in agricultural development. He shared stories of how drones had revolutionized farming practices, increasing crop yields and reducing environmental impact. However, he also highlighted the need for ethical guidelines to govern drone use and protect privacy rights.

Mr. Sibanda's work underscored the importance of ethical considerations in the adoption of emerging technologies. Chilufya and his team recognized the need for ethical impact assessments and community consultations to ensure that technology deployment was aligned with societal values and aspirations.

Inspired by Dr. Ngoma's vision and Mr. Sibanda's advocacy, Chilufya and his team returned to Kasama with a renewed sense of purpose. They convened a meeting under the baobab tree, inviting community leaders, residents, and technology experts to join them in discussing strategies for promoting ethical governance.

Chilufya shared the lessons from Lusaka and Mongu, illustrating the importance of placing ethics at the forefront of technology policymaking. He spoke of the need for ethical guidelines and codes of conduct to govern the use of technology in governance, and the importance of fostering a culture of ethical awareness and accountability. He emphasized the role of community engagement in shaping ethical governance practices that reflected the values and aspirations of society.

One of the local elders, Mrs. Mwamba, shared her perspective on the importance of ethics in governance. She spoke of the need for leaders to uphold integrity and honesty in their use of technology, and the responsibility of citizens to hold them accountable. "By embracing ethical governance practices, we can build a society that is just, fair, and inclusive," she declared, her voice filled with conviction.

The villagers nodded in agreement, their hearts stirred by the call to ethical action. They spoke of creating a community where technology was wielded with wisdom and integrity, where the rights and dignity of every individual were respected. They acknowledged the role of each person in upholding ethical governance principles and pledged to work together to implement the initiatives they had learned.

The local councilors pledged their support, promising to prioritize ethical considerations in their policymaking and implementation processes. They agreed to work hand in hand with the community, ensuring that every step they took toward ethical governance was a step toward a more just, transparent, and accountable society.

As the stars cast their gentle glow over the village, Chilufya stood before the gathered multitude. "We have learned that in the realm of governance, technology holds immense power, but with power comes responsibility," he declared, his voice echoing through the night. "Let us embark on this journey together, with humility and integrity, knowing that every step we take toward ethical governance is a step toward a brighter, more ethical future."

With unity in their hearts and purpose in their steps, Chilufya and his team set forth, their eyes fixed on the horizon where the promise of ethical governance awaited, their resolve unshakeable, their commitment unwavering—the guardians of integrity, the stewards of responsibility.

Chapter 14: International Relations and Diplomacy

Foreign Policy Objectives and Priorities

"Bridging Borders: Navigating Foreign Policy Objectives"

Under the sprawling branches of the revered baobab tree, the village of Kasama congregated once again. With a sense of reverence, Chilufya and his team delved into the realm of international relations and diplomacy. Tonight's focus illuminated the intricate dance of foreign policy objectives and priorities. Guided by the "Building Better Communities" handbook, they aimed to navigate the complexities of global diplomacy and forge meaningful connections with the wider world.

Chilufya's voice resonated with solemnity as he addressed the assembly. "In a world of interconnectedness, our relationships with other nations shape our destiny," he declared. "Tonight, let us explore how we can define and pursue our foreign policy objectives to advance the interests of our community and foster global cooperation."

To delve deeper into the realm of foreign policy objectives and priorities, Chilufya and his team embarked on a journey across Zambia, visiting communities that had grappled with the intricacies of international diplomacy. Their first stop was the bustling city of Ndola, where they met with Ambassador Kasonde, a seasoned diplomat with years of experience in representing Zambia's interests abroad.

In Ndola, they gained insights into the complexities of global politics and the importance of diplomacy in advancing national interests. Ambassador Kasonde shared stories of diplomatic negotiations and strategic alliances that had shaped Zambia's position on key global issues. Chilufya and his team marveled at the power of diplomacy to foster understanding and cooperation between nations.

Chilufya and his team were inspired by Ambassador Kasonde's wisdom and diplomatic acumen. They learned about the principles of sovereignty, non-interference, and peaceful coexistence that guided Zambia's foreign policy, and the importance of promoting regional integration and economic cooperation. The need for strategic foresight and flexibility in responding to global challenges became clear, as did the role of diplomacy in advancing national interests while upholding principles of justice and equality.

Next, the team explored Zambia's diplomatic priorities in the context of regional integration and economic development. They traveled to the border town of Livingstone, where they met with Dr. Mwape, a government official responsible for promoting cross-border trade and investment.

In Livingstone, they witnessed firsthand the benefits of

regional cooperation and economic integration. Dr. Mwape shared stories of how Zambia's participation in regional organizations such as the Southern African Development Community (SADC) had facilitated trade and investment flows, creating opportunities for economic growth and development. Chilufya and his team marveled at the power of regional diplomacy to build bridges between nations and unlock shared prosperity.

Inspired by Ambassador Kasonde's leadership and Dr. Mwape's vision, Chilufya and his team returned to Kasama with a renewed sense of purpose. They convened a meeting under the baobab tree, inviting community leaders, residents, and international experts to join them in discussing strategies for advancing Zambia's foreign policy objectives.

Chilufya shared the lessons from Ndola and Livingstone, illustrating the importance of diplomacy in advancing national interests and promoting global cooperation. He spoke of the need for Zambia to play an active role in regional and international fora, advocating for peace, security, and sustainable development. He emphasized the role of citizen diplomacy in fostering people-to-people ties and promoting cross-cultural understanding.

One of the local entrepreneurs, Mr. Banda, shared his perspective on the importance of international trade and investment for community development. He spoke of the opportunities presented by global markets and the need for Zambia to position itself as a competitive player on the world stage. "By pursuing our foreign policy objectives with vision and determination, we can create a better future for our community and the world," he declared, his voice filled with conviction.

The villagers nodded in agreement, their hearts stirred by the promise of global cooperation and mutual understanding. They spoke of creating a community where diversity was celebrated, where dialogue and diplomacy were valued, and where Zambia's voice was heard on the world stage. They acknowledged the role of each person in advancing Zambia's foreign policy objectives and pledged to work together to implement the initiatives they had learned.

The local councilors pledged their support, promising to prioritize diplomacy and international cooperation in their policymaking and advocacy efforts. They agreed to work hand in hand with the community, ensuring that every step they took toward advancing Zambia's foreign policy objectives was a step toward a more peaceful, prosperous, and interconnected world.

As the stars cast their gentle glow over the village, Chilufya stood before the gathered multitude. "We have learned that in a world of interconnectedness, our relationships with other nations shape our destiny," he declared, his voice echoing through the night. "Let us embark on this journey together, with courage and conviction, knowing that every step we take toward advancing Zambia's foreign policy objectives is a step toward a brighter, more peaceful future."

With unity in their hearts and purpose in their steps, Chilufya and his team set forth, their eyes fixed on the horizon where the promise of global cooperation awaited, their resolve unshakeable, their commitment unwavering—the architects of diplomacy, the ambassadors of peace.

Diplomatic Strategies and Negotiation Techniques

"Forging Bonds: The Art of Diplomatic Negotiation"

Beneath the majestic branches of the ancient baobab tree, the village of Kasama gathered once more, eager to delve into the intricate world of diplomacy and negotiation. With a sense of reverence, Chilufya and his team continued their exploration of international relations, focusing tonight on the delicate art of diplomatic strategies and negotiation techniques. Guided by the pages of the "Building Better Communities" handbook, they sought to unlock the secrets of forging strong bonds and fostering fruitful dialogue on the global stage.

Chilufya's voice carried a tone of determination as he addressed the assembly. "In the arena of diplomacy, strategic negotiation is the cornerstone of building bridges and fostering understanding between nations," he declared. "Tonight, let us explore the art of diplomatic negotiation and the strategies that underpin successful diplomatic endeavors."

To delve deeper into the realm of diplomatic strategies and negotiation techniques, Chilufya and his team embarked on a journey across Zambia, visiting communities that had honed the craft of diplomacy through centuries of interaction with neighboring nations. Their first stop was the bustling city of Kitwe, where they met with Chief Mwamba, a respected leader known for his skillful diplomacy in resolving disputes and forging alliances.

In Kitwe, they gained insights into the ancient traditions of diplomacy and negotiation that had guided Chief Mwamba's leadership. He shared stories of how diplomatic rituals and protocols had been used to foster peace and cooperation among rival tribes and neighboring kingdoms. Chilufya and his team marveled at the wisdom and foresight embedded in these time-honored practices.

Chilufya and his team were inspired by Chief Mwamba's mastery of diplomatic negotiation. They learned about the importance of patience, empathy, and cultural sensitivity in building trust and rapport with counterparts from different backgrounds. The need for strategic planning and flexibility in responding to changing circumstances became clear, as did the role of diplomacy in finding win-win solutions to complex problems.

Next, the team explored modern diplomatic strategies in the context of Zambia's engagement with regional and international partners. They traveled to the capital city of Lusaka, where they met with Ambassador Kabwe, a seasoned diplomat responsible for representing Zambia's interests in multilateral fora.

In Lusaka, they gained insights into the intricacies of modern diplomacy and the strategies employed by Ambassador Kabwe to advance Zambia's foreign policy objectives. He shared stories of how diplomatic alliances and coalitions had been leveraged to promote Zambia's interests on issues such as trade, security, and sustainable development. Chilufya and his team marveled at the complexity and sophistication of contemporary diplomatic engagements.

Inspired by Chief Mwamba's wisdom and Ambassador Kabwe's leadership, Chilufya and his team returned to Kasama with a renewed sense of purpose. They convened a meeting under the baobab tree, inviting community leaders, residents, and diplomatic experts to join them in discussing strategies for enhancing Zambia's diplomatic capabilities.

Chilufya shared the lessons from Kitwe and Lusaka, illustrating the importance of strategic negotiation in advancing Zambia's interests on the global stage. He spoke of the need for Zambia to develop a coherent and proactive diplomatic strategy that aligned with its national priorities and values. He emphasized the role of citizen diplomacy in supporting government efforts and building bridges of understanding between nations.

One of the local elders, Mrs. Sakala, shared her perspective on the importance of diplomacy in maintaining peace and stability in the region. She spoke of the need for Zambia to be a force for good in the world, advocating for justice, equality, and human rights. "By mastering the art of diplomatic negotiation, we can ensure that Zambia's voice is heard and respected on the global stage," she declared, her voice filled with conviction.

The villagers nodded in agreement, their hearts stirred by the call to diplomatic action. They spoke of creating a community where diplomacy was valued as a tool for peace and prosperity, where dialogue and negotiation were seen as pathways to understanding and cooperation. They acknowledged the role of each person in supporting Zambia's diplomatic efforts and pledged to work together to implement the initiatives they had learned.

The local councilors pledged their support, promising to prioritize diplomatic training and capacity building in their policymaking and advocacy efforts. They agreed to work hand in hand with the community, ensuring that every step they took toward enhancing Zambia's diplomatic capabilities was a step toward a more peaceful, prosperous, and interconnected world.

As the stars cast their gentle glow over the village, Chilufya stood before the gathered multitude. "We have learned that in the arena of diplomacy, strategic negotiation is the cornerstone of building bridges and fostering understanding between nations," he declared, his voice echoing through the night. "Let us embark on this journey together, with wisdom and humility, knowing that every step we take toward mastering the art of diplomatic negotiation is a step toward a brighter, more harmonious future."

With unity in their hearts and purpose in their steps, Chilufya and his team set forth, their eyes fixed on the horizon where the promise of diplomatic success awaited, their resolve unshakeable, their commitment unwavering—the architects of peace, the ambassadors of goodwill.

International Development Cooperation

"Unity in Diversity: Navigating International Development Cooperation"

Underneath the sprawling canopy of the revered baobab tree, the village of Kasama gathered once more, eager to continue their exploration into the realm of international relations and diplomacy. With reverence, Chilufya and his team delved deeper into the complexities of global cooperation, focusing tonight on the vital aspect of international development cooperation. Guided by the wisdom within the "Building Better Communities" handbook, they aimed to unravel the intricacies of forging bonds across borders and fostering unity amidst diversity.

Chilufya's voice resonated with solemnity as he addressed

the assembly. "In the tapestry of global affairs, international development cooperation serves as the thread that binds nations together in pursuit of shared prosperity and progress," he declared. "Tonight, let us explore the significance of international development cooperation and the role it plays in shaping our collective future."

To delve deeper into the realm of international development cooperation, Chilufya and his team embarked on a journey across Zambia, visiting communities that had benefited from the support of international partners. Their first stop was the rural village of Kasama, where they met with Mr. Ng'andu, a community leader who had spearheaded a development project funded by an international aid organization.

In Kasama, they witnessed firsthand the transformative impact of international development cooperation on the lives of ordinary people. Mr. Ng'andu shared stories of how the project had improved access to clean water, healthcare, and education, lifting families out of poverty and empowering communities to build a brighter future. Chilufya and his team marveled at the power of partnership and solidarity to drive positive change.

Chilufya and his team were inspired by Mr. Ng'andu's dedication to his community and the spirit of collaboration that underpinned the development project. They learned about the importance of mutual respect, trust, and transparency in fostering effective partnerships between donors and recipients. The need for inclusive and sustainable development approaches that prioritized local ownership and participation became clear, as did the role of international development cooperation in advancing the global goals of peace, prosperity, and sustainable development.

Next, the team explored Zambia's role as a recipient and provider of international development assistance. They traveled to the capital city of Lusaka, where they met with Ms. Banda, a government official responsible for coordinating Zambia's development cooperation efforts with international partners.

In Lusaka, they gained insights into Zambia's engagement with the international community and the principles that guided its approach to development cooperation. Ms. Banda shared stories of how Zambia had benefited from the support of international partners in areas such as infrastructure development, health, and education, while also contributing to regional and global initiatives aimed at addressing poverty, inequality, and climate change. Chilufya and his team marveled at the spirit of solidarity and cooperation that underpinned Zambia's engagement with the international community.

Inspired by Mr. Ng'andu's grassroots leadership and Ms. Banda's diplomatic acumen, Chilufya and his team returned to Kasama with a renewed sense of purpose. They convened a meeting under the baobab tree, inviting community leaders, residents, and representatives from international organizations to join them in discussing strategies for enhancing Zambia's engagement in international development cooperation.

Chilufya shared the lessons from Kasama and Lusaka, illustrating the importance of international development cooperation in driving sustainable development and poverty reduction. He spoke of the need for Zambia to leverage its partnerships with international donors, civil society organizations, and the private sector to maximize the impact of development interventions. He emphasized the role of community engagement in shaping development priorities and ensuring that no one was left behind in the pursuit of shared prosperity.

One of the local farmers, Mr. Simbeye, shared his perspective on the importance of international cooperation in addressing global challenges such as climate change and food security. He spoke of the opportunities presented by international partnerships for sharing knowledge, technology, and resources to build resilience and promote sustainable development. "By working together with our international partners, we can achieve far more than we ever could alone," he declared, his voice filled with conviction.

The villagers nodded in agreement, their hearts stirred by the vision of a world united in pursuit of common goals. They spoke of creating a community where solidarity and cooperation transcended borders, where diversity was celebrated as a source of strength, and where every individual had the opportunity to thrive. They acknowledged the role of each person in advancing Zambia's engagement in international development cooperation and pledged to work together to implement the initiatives they had learned.

The local councilors pledged their support, promising to prioritize development cooperation in their policymaking and resource allocation efforts. They agreed to work hand in hand with the community, ensuring that every step they took toward enhancing Zambia's engagement in international development cooperation was a step toward a more just, equitable, and sustainable world.

As the stars cast their gentle glow over the village, Chilufya stood before the gathered multitude. "We have learned that in the tapestry of global affairs, international development cooperation serves as the thread that binds nations together in pursuit of shared prosperity and progress," he declared, his voice echoing through the night. "Let us embark on this journey together, with open hearts and

Humanitarian Assistance and Disaster Relief

"Hands Across Borders: Humanity in Action"

Beneath the majestic baobab tree, the heart of Kasama pulsed with anticipation as Chilufya and his team continued their odyssey through international relations. Tonight's focus was on the humanitarian imperative that transcended borders, bringing solace in times of crisis and hope amidst despair. Guided by the pages of the "Building Better Communities" handbook, they sought to unravel the essence of humanitarian assistance and disaster relief, weaving threads of compassion into the fabric of their collective journey.

Chilufya's voice, a beacon of empathy, resonated through the gathering. "In the tapestry of humanity, the threads of compassion bind us all," he declared. "Tonight, let us explore the profound impact of humanitarian assistance and disaster relief, as we extend our hands across borders to uplift those in need."

To delve deeper into the realm of humanitarian assistance and disaster relief, Chilufya and his team embarked on a journey across Zambia, visiting communities that had witnessed the transformative power of international solidarity in times of crisis. Their first stop was the flood-ravaged town of Mongu, where they met with Mrs. Kambole, a resilient community leader who had led relief efforts during the recent disaster.

In Mongu, they bore witness to the devastation wrought by nature's fury and the indomitable spirit of resilience that rose to meet it. Mrs. Kambole shared stories of how international aid organizations had rushed to the town's aid, providing emergency shelter, food, and medical assistance to those displaced by the floods. Chilufya and his team marveled at the outpouring of compassion and solidarity that had transcended borders to offer solace in the face of adversity.

Chilufya and his team were deeply moved by Mrs. Kambole's courage and the generosity of spirit that had defined the town's response to the disaster. They learned about the principles of neutrality, impartiality, and humanity that underpinned humanitarian assistance, and the importance of coordination and collaboration in delivering aid effectively. The need for long-term recovery and resilience-building efforts that empowered communities to withstand future disasters became clear, as did the role of humanitarian assistance in upholding the dignity and rights of those affected by crises.

Next, the team explored Zambia's role as both a recipient and provider of humanitarian assistance and disaster relief. They traveled to the bustling city of Ndola, where they met with Mr. Mulenga, a government official responsible for coordinating Zambia's response to emergencies and disasters.

In Ndola, they gained insights into Zambia's preparedness and response mechanisms for disasters, and the partnerships that enabled it to provide assistance to neighboring countries in times of need. Mr. Mulenga shared stories of Zambia's contributions to regional and international relief efforts, from providing shelter to refugees fleeing conflict to offering medical assistance to countries devastated by natural disasters. Chilufya and his team marveled at the spirit of solidarity and generosity that had characterized Zambia's humanitarian engagements.

Inspired by Mrs. Kambole's resilience and Mr. Mulenga's leadership, Chilufya and his team returned to Kasama with a renewed sense of purpose. They convened a meeting under the baobab tree, inviting community leaders, residents, and representatives from international humanitarian organizations to join them in discussing strategies for enhancing Zambia's engagement in humanitarian assistance and disaster relief.

Chilufya shared the lessons from Mongu and Ndola, illustrating the importance of compassion and solidarity in times of crisis, and the role of humanitarian assistance in alleviating suffering and building resilience. He spoke of the need for Zambia to strengthen its preparedness and response mechanisms for disasters, and to prioritize the needs of the most vulnerable in its humanitarian interventions. He emphasized the role of community-based approaches in disaster risk reduction and management, and the importance of building partnerships with local organizations and communities to ensure a coordinated and effective response.

One of the local nurses, Ms. Chanda, shared her perspective on the importance of humanitarian assistance in saving lives and alleviating suffering. She spoke of the profound impact that international support had on her community during times of crisis, and the hope it brought to those who had lost everything. "By extending our hands across borders in times of need, we demonstrate the best of humanity and sow seeds of hope for a brighter future," she declared, her voice filled with conviction.

The villagers nodded in agreement, their hearts filled

with compassion and solidarity. They spoke of creating a community where no one was left behind in times of crisis, where compassion knew no borders, and where every individual had the support and solidarity of a global family. They acknowledged the role of each person in extending a helping hand to those in need, and pledged to work together to implement the initiatives they had learned.

The local councilors pledged their support, promising to prioritize humanitarian assistance and disaster relief in their policymaking and resource allocation efforts. They agreed to work hand in hand with the community, ensuring that every step they took toward enhancing Zambia's engagement in humanitarian assistance and disaster relief was a step toward a more compassionate, resilient, and inclusive world.

As the stars

Peacebuilding and Conflict Resolution Efforts

"Harmony Amidst Strife: The Quest for Peace"

In the tranquil shade of the age-old baobab tree, the village of Kasama gathered once more, eager to unravel the intricacies of international relations. Tonight, Chilufya and his team delved into the profound pursuit of peacebuilding and conflict resolution, seeking to understand the delicate balance between discord and harmony in the global arena. Guided by the "Building Better Communities" handbook, they embarked on a journey to illuminate pathways to peace amidst the tumult of conflict.

With a solemn tone, Chilufya addressed the assembly, "In the tapestry of humanity, peace is the thread that binds us together, weaving a fabric of understanding and cooperation." Tonight, they would explore the intricate art of peacebuilding and conflict resolution, delving into the depths of human resilience and diplomacy.

Their journey led them first to the war-torn region of Kapiri Mposhi, where they met with Chief Chanda, a revered leader known for his tireless efforts in mediating conflicts and fostering reconciliation among warring factions. Amidst the scars of conflict, Chief Chanda's unwavering resolve offered a beacon of hope, a testament to the human spirit's capacity for forgiveness and healing.

Chilufya and his team were humbled by Chief Chanda's wisdom and the profound impact of his peacebuilding efforts. They learned about the importance of dialogue, empathy, and inclusivity in resolving conflicts and building sustainable peace. The need for community-led reconciliation processes that addressed the root causes of violence and injustice became clear, as did the role of international support in facilitating peace negotiations and post-conflict reconstruction.

Next, the team explored Zambia's role as a mediator and peacekeeper in regional conflicts. They traveled to the bustling city of Chipata, where they met with Colonel Banda, a military officer who had served in peacekeeping missions across Africa. Colonel Banda shared stories of Zambia's contributions to peacekeeping efforts, from deploying troops to conflict zones to providing training and logistical support to regional peacekeeping operations.

In Chipata, they gained insights into the complexities of peacekeeping and the challenges of navigating fragile post-conflict environments. Colonel Banda emphasized the importance of impartiality, professionalism, and respect for human rights in peacekeeping missions, and the need for sustained international engagement to support peacebuilding and reconciliation efforts. Chilufya and his team marveled at the courage and dedication of Zambia's peacekeepers, who risked their lives to bring hope and stability to war-torn regions.

Inspired by Chief Chanda's compassion and Colonel Banda's bravery, Chilufya and his team returned to Kasama with a renewed sense of purpose. They convened a meeting under the baobab tree, inviting community leaders, residents, and representatives from international peacekeeping organizations to join them in discussing strategies for enhancing Zambia's engagement in peacebuilding and conflict resolution.

Chilufya shared the lessons from Kapiri Mposhi and Chipata, illustrating the importance of peacebuilding in creating a more just and peaceful world. He spoke of the need for Zambia to leverage its experience and expertise in conflict resolution to promote peace and stability in the region and beyond. He emphasized the role of community-based initiatives in addressing the root causes of conflict and building social cohesion and resilience.

One of the local teachers, Mr. Mwamba, shared his perspective on the importance of peacebuilding in creating a better future for the next generation. He spoke of the profound impact that peace and stability had on children's lives, allowing them to grow up in safety and pursue their dreams. "By investing in peacebuilding and conflict resolution, we invest in the future of our children and generations to come," he declared, his voice filled with conviction.

The villagers nodded in agreement, their hearts stirred

by the vision of a world free from violence and fear. They spoke of creating a community where conflicts were resolved through dialogue and understanding, where forgiveness and reconciliation prevailed over hatred and division. They acknowledged the role of each person in promoting peace and pledged to work together to implement the initiatives they had learned.

The local councilors pledged their support, promising to prioritize peacebuilding and conflict resolution in their policymaking and resource allocation efforts. They agreed to work hand in hand with the community, ensuring that every step they took toward enhancing Zambia's engagement in peacebuilding and conflict resolution was a step toward a more peaceful, just, and sustainable world.

As the stars cast their gentle glow over the village, Chilufya stood before the gathered multitude. "We have learned that in the tapestry of humanity, peace is the thread that binds us together," he declared, his voice echoing through the night. "Let us embark on this journey together, with compassion and courage, knowing that every step we take toward peacebuilding and conflict resolution is a step toward a brighter, more harmonious future."

With unity in their hearts and purpose in their steps, Chilufya and his

Global Governance and Multilateralism

"Bridging Nations: The Power of Global Governance"

Beneath the sprawling branches of the baobab tree, the village of Kasama convened once more, eager to explore the intricate webs of global governance and multilateralism. Tonight, Chilufya and his team embarked on a quest to unravel the complexities of international cooperation, weaving threads of unity and cooperation across borders. Guided by the wisdom within the "Building Better Communities" handbook, they sought to illuminate pathways to collective action and global solidarity.

With a sense of purpose, Chilufya addressed the assembly, "In the tapestry of global affairs, the bonds of cooperation transcend borders, fostering unity amidst diversity." Tonight, they would delve into the realm of global governance and multilateralism, exploring the mechanisms that underpinned international cooperation and collective action.

Their journey led them first to the bustling city of Livingstone, where they met with Ms. Sampa, a seasoned diplomat who had represented Zambia at the United Nations. Amidst the towering Victoria Falls, Ms. Sampa shared insights into the intricacies of global governance, highlighting the role of international organizations in addressing shared challenges and advancing common goals.

Chilufya and his team were captivated by Ms. Sampa's tales of diplomacy and negotiation on the world stage. They learned about the principles of multilateralism, cooperation, and diplomacy that underpinned global governance, and the importance of institutions such as the United Nations in promoting peace, security, and sustainable development. The need for inclusive and effective global governance mechanisms that reflected the diversity of the international community became clear, as did the role of Zambia in shaping the global agenda.

Next, the team explored Zambia's engagement with regional and international organizations, from the African Union to the World Trade Organization. They traveled to the capital city of Lusaka, where they met with Mr. Mwanza, a government official responsible for coordinating Zambia's participation in multilateral forums.

In Lusaka, they gained insights into Zambia's contributions to global governance and the partnerships that enabled it to influence international decision-making processes. Mr. Mwanza shared stories of Zambia's advocacy for African interests on the global stage, from promoting peace and security to advancing economic development and environmental sustainability. Chilufya and his team marveled at the power of collective action and solidarity to address shared challenges and opportunities.

Inspired by Ms. Sampa's diplomacy and Mr. Mwanza's leadership, Chilufya and his team returned to Kasama with a renewed sense of purpose. They convened a meeting under the baobab tree, inviting community leaders, residents, and representatives from international organizations to join them in discussing strategies for enhancing Zambia's engagement in global governance and multilateralism.

Chilufya shared the lessons from Livingstone and Lusaka, illustrating the importance of global governance in addressing global challenges and advancing shared interests. He spoke of the need for Zambia to leverage its diplomatic capabilities and regional leadership to shape the global agenda and promote the interests of the African continent. He emphasized the role of civil society and youth in advocating for meaningful participation in global governance processes and holding international institutions accountable.

One of the local entrepreneurs, Ms. Ngoma, shared her perspective on the importance of global governance in creating an enabling environment for business and innovation. She spoke of the opportunities presented by international trade agreements and investment treaties for promoting economic growth and development. "By engaging actively in global governance," she declared, "we can create a more just, equitable, and prosperous world for future generations."

The villagers nodded in agreement, their hearts filled with hope and determination. They spoke of creating a community where every voice was heard and every perspective valued in the global dialogue, where solidarity and cooperation prevailed over division and discord. They acknowledged the role of each person in shaping the future of global governance and pledged to work together to implement the initiatives they had learned.

The local councilors pledged their support, promising to prioritize global governance and multilateralism in their policymaking and advocacy efforts. They agreed to work hand in hand with the community, ensuring that every step they took toward enhancing Zambia's engagement in global governance was a step toward a more peaceful, prosperous, and sustainable world.

As the stars cast their gentle glow over the village, Chilufya stood before the gathered multitude. "We have learned that in the tapestry of global affairs, the bonds of cooperation transcend borders," he declared, his voice echoing through the night. "Let us embark on this journey together, with unity and purpose, knowing that every step we take toward global governance and multilateralism is a step toward a brighter, more interconnected future."

With unity in their hearts and purpose in their steps, Chilufya and his team embraced the challenges and opportunities of global governance, their resolve unshakeable, their vision clear—the architects of a more just and equitable world, bound by the ties of solidarity and cooperation.

15

Chapter 15: Future Trends and Challenges in Public Policy

Anticipating and Adapting to Technological Disruptions

"Navigating the Future: Adapting to Technological Disruptions"

Under the ancient baobab tree, the villagers of Kasama gathered once more, their faces reflecting a mix of curiosity and concern. Chilufya and his team were ready to tackle another pressing issue from the "Building Better Communities" handbook: anticipating and adapting to technological disruptions. This evening, they would explore the impact of rapid technological change on their community and strategize ways to navigate these disruptions effectively.

Chilufya began with a sense of urgency in his voice, "In our rapidly changing world, technology evolves at an unprecedented pace. To build a resilient community, we must anticipate these changes and adapt our policies accordingly." Tonight, they would delve into the potential disruptions posed by technological advancements and the strategies needed to adapt and thrive.

Their journey started in the bustling city of Lusaka, where they visited the Zambian Institute of Technology. Here, they met with Professor Mwila, an expert in technology and innovation. Amidst the hum of futuristic gadgets and the glow of interactive displays, Professor Mwila introduced them to the concept of technological disruptions and their impact on society.

Chilufya and his team listened intently as Professor Mwila explained how advancements in artificial intelligence, robotics, and biotechnology could transform various sectors, from healthcare and education to agriculture and manufacturing. They learned about the potential for job displacement due to automation and the need for new skill sets in the workforce. The importance of proactive policy measures to address these challenges was emphasized.

Next, the team journeyed to the industrial hub of Ndola, where they met with Mr. Banda, a business leader at the forefront of integrating new technologies into his manufacturing operations. In the midst of humming machines and busy workers, Mr. Banda shared his experiences of navigating technological disruptions. He spoke of the benefits and challenges of automation and the need for continuous learning and adaptation.

In Ndola, Chilufya and his team witnessed firsthand the impact of technological disruptions on industry and employment. They saw how businesses were adopting new technologies to improve efficiency and competitiveness, but also noted the concerns of workers about job security and the need for retraining. Mr. Banda emphasized the importance of partnerships between government, industry, and educational institutions to prepare the workforce for the future.

Inspired by the insights from Lusaka and Ndola, Chilufya and his team returned to Kasama with a sense of urgency and determination. They convened a meeting under the baobab tree, inviting community leaders, residents, and technology experts to discuss strategies for anticipating and adapting to technological disruptions.

Chilufya shared the lessons learned, emphasizing the need for a proactive approach to policy making. He spoke of the importance of investing in education and training programs to equip the workforce with the skills needed for the future. He highlighted the role of innovation and entrepreneurship in creating new opportunities and mitigating the impact of job displacement.

One of the local artisans, Mrs. Mulenga, expressed her concerns about the impact of automation on traditional crafts and employment. She spoke of the need for policies that supported small businesses and encouraged innovation in the local economy. "By embracing change and adapting our skills," she declared, "we can ensure that our community thrives in the face of technological disruptions."

The villagers nodded in agreement, their hearts filled with resolve. They spoke of creating a community where technology was seen as an opportunity rather than a threat. They acknowledged the role of each person in shaping a resilient and adaptable future and pledged to work together to implement the strategies they had discussed.

The local councilors pledged their support, promising to

prioritize investments in education, training, and innovation. They agreed to work collaboratively with the community, ensuring that every step taken toward anticipating and adapting to technological disruptions was a step toward a more resilient and prosperous society.

As the stars cast their gentle glow over the village, Chilufya stood before the gathered multitude. "We have learned that in our rapidly changing world, technology evolves at an unprecedented pace," he declared, his voice resonating with conviction. "Let us embrace the future with open hearts and minds, navigating the disruptions with resilience and innovation."

With unity in their hearts and purpose in their steps, Chilufya and his team embraced the challenge of adapting to technological disruptions, their resolve unyielding. They knew that the journey ahead would be complex, but their commitment to building a resilient and adaptable community would guide them every step of the way.

Addressing Global Health Pandemics

"Guardians of Health: Confronting the Invisible Enemy"

Under the ancient baobab tree, the villagers of Kasama gathered once more, their faces illuminated by the flickering flames of the communal fire. As they faced the daunting task of addressing global health pandemics, Chilufya and his team stood ready to guide them through this critical journey, drawing upon the insights of the "Building Better Communities" handbook. Together, they prepared to confront the invisible enemy with wisdom, unity, and resilience.

With a solemn air, Chilufya began, "In the vast tapestry of life, pandemics strike with a swiftness and ferocity that can leave communities shattered. Yet, it is within our power to rise above these challenges, to protect and heal." Tonight, their mission was to understand and combat the threat of global health pandemics.

Their journey led them first to the bustling city of Lusaka, where they met with Dr. Kunda, an epidemiologist renowned for his work on infectious diseases. Amidst the sterile, high-tech environment of a research lab, Dr. Kunda shared stories of battling past pandemics, from HIV/AIDS to Ebola to COVID-19, and the crucial lessons learned in the process.

Chilufya and his team listened intently as Dr. Kunda spoke of the importance of surveillance systems, rapid response teams, and international cooperation. They learned about the essential role of vaccines, the necessity of robust healthcare infrastructure, and the critical need for global equity in healthcare access. The magnitude of the task was daunting, but the path forward became clearer: preparedness, vigilance, and solidarity were key.

Next, the team traveled to the rural village of Chipata, where they met with Nurse Mwansa, who had tirelessly served her community through the peaks of various health crises. In the modest confines of a local clinic, Nurse Mwansa shared her firsthand experiences of dealing with outbreaks and the vital importance of community trust and education.

In Chipata, they saw the challenges of delivering healthcare in resource-limited settings and the resilience of frontline workers. Nurse Mwansa emphasized the need for clear communication, local engagement, and the building of trust within communities to combat misinformation and fear. Chilufya and his team were inspired by the dedication and bravery of healthcare workers like Nurse Mwansa, understanding that combating pandemics required a collective effort.

Armed with insights from Lusaka and Chipata, Chilufya and his team returned to Kasama, determined to fortify their community against future pandemics. They convened a meeting under the baobab tree, inviting community leaders, residents, and health sector representatives to discuss strategies for pandemic preparedness and response.

Chilufya shared the lessons learned, stressing the importance of building robust healthcare systems, ensuring equitable access to medical resources, and fostering international cooperation. He spoke of the need for community-driven approaches, where local knowledge and leadership played pivotal roles in pandemic response efforts.

One of the local health volunteers, Mr. Musonda, spoke passionately about the need for grassroots mobilization and health education. He emphasized the power of community networks in disseminating accurate information and supporting public health measures. "By working together and supporting one another," he declared, "we can build a community that is resilient in the face of any health crisis."

The villagers nodded in agreement, their hearts filled with resolve. They spoke of creating a community where health was a shared responsibility, where no one was left behind, and where every individual had access to the care and support they needed. They acknowledged the role of each person in shaping the future of public health and pledged to work together to implement the strategies they had discussed.

The local councilors pledged their support, promising to prioritize health policies and investments that strengthened public health infrastructure and promoted community resilience. They agreed to work collaboratively with the community, ensuring that every step taken toward addressing global health pandemics was a step toward a healthier and more united future.

As the stars cast their gentle glow over the village, Chilufya stood before the gathered multitude. "We have learned that in the vast tapestry of life, our greatest strength lies in our unity and compassion," he declared, his voice resonating with conviction. "Let us stand together as guardians of health, ready to confront and overcome any challenge that comes our way."

With unity in their hearts and purpose in their steps, Chilufya and his team embraced the challenge of global health pandemics, determined to build a future where their community would not only survive but thrive amidst adversity.

Climate Change and Environmental Sustainability

"Guardians of the Earth: Preserving Our Planet Amidst Change"

Beneath the sprawling branches of the ancient baobab tree, the villagers of Kasama gathered once more, their spirits unwavering as they ventured into the realm of climate change and environmental sustainability. Led by Chilufya and his team, they embarked on a quest to safeguard their planet against the ravages of climate change, guided by the wisdom within the "Building Better Communities" handbook. Together, they prepared to confront the daunting challenges of environmental degradation with courage and determination.

With a solemn reverence, Chilufya addressed the assembly, "In the tapestry of nature, the winds of change blow fierce and unyielding—the specter of climate change looms large over our world." Tonight, they would embark on a journey to confront this existential threat, to unravel its mysteries and forge a path towards environmental sustainability and resilience.

Their odyssey began with a pilgrimage to the heart of ecological wisdom in the rural village of Chinsali, where they met with Elder Mwamba, a venerable guardian of the land. Amidst the whispering leaves of ancient trees, Elder Mwamba shared tales of harmony and balance, and the sacred bond between humanity and nature.

Chilufya and his team were enraptured by Elder Mwamba's wisdom, learning of the delicate balance of ecosystems and the profound impacts of human activities on the environment. They discovered the interconnectedness of all life forms and the urgent need for sustainable practices that preserved biodiversity and mitigated climate change. The imperative of protecting natural resources, promoting renewable energy, and fostering ecological stewardship became abundantly clear, as did the role of communities in driving positive change.

Next, the team journeyed to the bustling city of Ndola, where they met with Ms. Banda, a visionary environmentalist leading the charge for sustainability. In the midst of bustling streets and towering skyscrapers, Ms. Banda shared stories of resilience and innovation in the face of environmental challenges, and visions of a future where cities and nature coexisted in harmony.

In Ndola, they witnessed the impacts of urbanization and industrialization on the environment, and the importance of sustainable development in mitigating climate change. Ms. Banda emphasized the need for green infrastructure, sustainable transportation, and circular economy practices to reduce carbon emissions and promote resilience in urban areas. Chilufya and his team marveled at the ingenuity and determination of environmental activists, and the urgent need for collective action and systemic change.

Inspired by Elder Mwamba's wisdom and Ms. Banda's leadership, Chilufya and his team returned to Kasama with a renewed sense of purpose. They convened a meeting under the baobab tree, inviting community leaders, residents, and representatives from the environmental sector to join them in discussing strategies for addressing climate change and promoting environmental sustainability.

Chilufya shared the lessons from Chinsali and Ndola, illustrating the importance of ecological stewardship and sustainable development in confronting climate change. He spoke of the need for transformative policies and investments to promote renewable energy, protect ecosystems, and build resilience to climate impacts. He emphasized the role of community engagement and empowerment in driving sustainable development at the local level.

One of the local conservationists, Mr. Sichalwe, shared his perspective on the importance of grassroots mobilization and environmental education in promoting environmental sustainability. He spoke of the resilience of nature and the urgency of collective action in preserving the planet for future generations. "By working together as stewards of the earth," he declared, "we can overcome even the greatest of challenges and forge a path towards a more sustainable and resilient future."

The villagers nodded in agreement, their hearts filled with determination and solidarity. They spoke of creating a community where nature was revered as a sacred gift, where every action was guided by principles of sustainability and respect for the earth. They acknowledged the role of each person in shaping the future of environmental policy and pledged to work together to implement the initiatives they had learned.

The local councilors pledged their support, promising to prioritize policies and investments that promoted environmental sustainability and resilience in their policymaking and resource allocation efforts. They agreed to work hand in hand with the community, ensuring that every step they took toward addressing climate change and promoting environmental sustainability was a step toward a healthier, more resilient, and harmonious world.

As the stars cast their gentle glow over the village, Chilufya stood before the gathered multitude. "We have learned that in the tapestry of nature, the winds of change blow fierce and unyielding," he declared, his voice resonating with conviction. "Let us stand together as guardians of the earth, forging a path towards a future where nature thrives, and all life flourishes in harmony."

With unity in their hearts and purpose in their steps, Chilufya and his team embraced the challenges of climate change and environmental sustainability, their resolve unyielding. They knew that the journey ahead would be arduous, but their commitment to preserving the planet and building a sustainable future would guide them every step of the way.

Social and Economic Inequality

"Bridging the Divide: Addressing Inequality for a Better Tomorrow"

Under the sprawling branches of the ancient baobab tree, the villagers of Kasama gathered once more, their hearts and minds set on the pressing issue of social and economic inequality. Guided by Chilufya and his team, they prepared to confront the disparities that threatened to fracture their community. Drawing upon the wisdom within the "Building Better Communities" handbook, they sought to build a future where everyone had the opportunity to thrive.

Chilufya began with a solemn tone, "In the fabric of our society, inequality is a tear that weakens us all. To build a stronger, more resilient community, we must bridge these divides and ensure that every individual has the chance to prosper." Tonight, their mission was to understand the roots of inequality and explore ways to address it effectively.

Their journey started in the bustling town of Kitwe, where they met with Professor Lungu, an expert in social policy and economic development. Amidst the hum of industry and commerce, Professor Lungu shared his insights on the systemic issues that perpetuate inequality, from education and employment disparities to access to healthcare and housing.

Chilufya and his team listened intently as Professor Lungu explained the interconnectedness of social and economic factors. They learned about the importance of inclusive economic policies that targeted marginalized communities and the need for comprehensive social safety nets. The imperative of education, healthcare access, and fair labor practices became clear as crucial elements in addressing inequality.

Next, the team traveled to the serene village of Mpulungu on the shores of Lake Tanganyika, where they met with Mama Tembo, a respected community leader and advocate for women's rights. In the peaceful setting of her home, Mama Tembo shared her experiences of working with disadvantaged groups, emphasizing the need for grassroots empowerment and community-led initiatives.

In Mpulungu, they saw the challenges faced by women and other marginalized groups in accessing opportunities and resources. Mama Tembo spoke passionately about the importance of gender equality and the role of women in driving economic and social progress. She highlighted the need for policies that supported women's participation in the workforce, provided access to education and healthcare, and protected against discrimination and violence.

Armed with insights from Kitwe and Mpulungu, Chilufya and his team returned to Kasama, determined to address the inequalities within their own community. They convened a meeting under the baobab tree, inviting community leaders, residents, and representatives from various sectors to discuss strategies for promoting social and economic equality.

Chilufya shared the lessons learned, emphasizing the importance of inclusive policies and community engagement in addressing inequality. He spoke of the need for targeted interventions that provided education, healthcare, and economic opportunities to marginalized groups. He highlighted the role of social safety nets in protecting vulnerable populations and promoting economic mobility.

One of the local youth leaders, Bwalya, spoke passionately about the need for equal access to education and employment opportunities. He emphasized the importance of youth empowerment and the role of young people in driving social change. "By investing in our youth and ensuring that everyone has the opportunity to succeed," he declared, "we can build a community that is strong, inclusive, and resilient."

The villagers nodded in agreement, their hearts filled with resolve. They spoke of creating a community where everyone, regardless of their background, had the chance to thrive. They acknowledged the role of each person in shaping a more equitable future and pledged to work together to implement the strategies they had discussed.

The local councilors pledged their support, promising to prioritize policies and investments that promoted social and economic equality. They agreed to work collaboratively with the community, ensuring that every step taken toward addressing inequality was a step toward a more just and prosperous society.

As the stars cast their gentle glow over the village, Chilufya stood before the gathered multitude. "We have learned that in the fabric of our society, inequality is a tear that weakens us all," he declared, his voice resonating with conviction. "Let us stand together as builders of bridges, forging a path toward a future where everyone has the opportunity to prosper."

With unity in their hearts and purpose in their steps, Chilufya and his team embraced the challenge of social and economic inequality, their resolve unyielding. They knew that the journey ahead would be difficult, but their commitment to building a more equitable and inclusive community would guide them every step of the way.

Political Polarization and Democratic Governance

"Uniting the Divide: Navigating Political Polarization for a Stronger Democracy"

Chilufya began with a tone of solemnity in his voice, "In our community and beyond, political polarization threatens the very fabric of our democracy. To build a stronger society, we must find ways to bridge our differences and govern with unity." Tonight, they would embark on a journey to understand the roots of political polarization and the importance of democratic governance in overcoming these challenges.

Their exploration started in the capital city of Lusaka, where they visited the National Assembly. Here, they met with Honorable Ms. Chanda, a seasoned politician known for her efforts to foster bipartisan cooperation. Amidst the echoing halls of parliament, Honorable Chanda shared her experiences of navigating the polarized political landscape and the importance of dialogue and compromise in democratic governance.

Chilufya and his team listened intently as Honorable Chanda explained how political polarization could lead to gridlock, undermine trust in institutions, and erode the democratic process. She emphasized the need for politicians to prioritize the common good over partisan interests and highlighted successful initiatives where cross-party collaboration had led to meaningful reforms.

Next, the team journeyed to the town of Livingstone, where they met with Mr. Kabwe, a community leader who had facilitated numerous local dialogues aimed at bridging political divides. In the heart of the vibrant town, Mr. Kabwe shared his experiences of bringing together individuals from different political backgrounds to discuss common concerns and find shared solutions.

In Livingstone, Chilufya and his team witnessed firsthand the impact of grassroots initiatives in reducing political polarization. They saw how open dialogue, mutual respect, and a focus on common goals could foster understanding and cooperation among community members. Mr. Kabwe emphasized the importance of creating safe spaces for conversation and the role of civil society in promoting democratic values.

Inspired by the insights from Lusaka and Livingstone, Chilufya and his team returned to Mwinilunga with a renewed commitment to fostering unity and democratic governance. They convened a meeting under the baobab tree, inviting community leaders, residents, and representatives from various political groups to discuss strategies for overcoming political polarization.

Chilufya shared the lessons learned, emphasizing the need for open dialogue and collaboration. He spoke of the importance of focusing on shared values and common goals rather than partisan differences. He highlighted the role of education in promoting democratic values and critical thinking, as well as the need for transparency and accountability in governance.

One of the local farmers, Mr. Tembo, expressed his concerns about the impact of political polarization on community development. He spoke of the need for policies that addressed the needs of all residents, regardless of political affiliation. "By working together and prioritizing the common good," he declared, "we can build a stronger, more united community."

The villagers nodded in agreement, their hearts filled with

resolve. They spoke of creating a community where political differences were respected, and common goals were pursued with unity and determination. They acknowledged the role of each person in fostering a healthy democratic process and pledged to work together to implement the strategies they had discussed.

The local councilors pledged their support, promising to prioritize initiatives that promoted dialogue, transparency, and accountability. They agreed to work collaboratively with the community, ensuring that every step taken toward overcoming political polarization was a step toward a more democratic and united society.

As the stars cast their gentle glow over the village, Chilufya stood before the gathered multitude. "We have learned that political polarization threatens the very fabric of our democracy," he declared, his voice resonating with conviction. "Let us embrace the spirit of dialogue and unity, working together to strengthen our democratic governance."

With unity in their hearts and purpose in their steps, Chilufya and his team embraced the challenge of overcoming political polarization, their resolve unyielding. They knew that the journey ahead would be complex, but their commitment to fostering a strong, democratic community would guide them every step of the way.

The Role of Artificial Intelligence in Policy Making

"Embracing the Future: Harnessing AI for Better Policy Making"

Under the ancient baobab tree, the villagers of Kasama gathered once more, their faces alight with curiosity and anticipation. Chilufya and his team stood ready to explore the final subpoint of their journey: the role of artificial intelligence in policy making. This evening, they would delve into the possibilities and challenges of integrating AI into the policy-making process, guided by the wisdom within the "Building Better Communities" handbook.

Chilufya began with a sense of wonder in his voice, "In the realm of technology, we stand on the brink of a new era. Artificial intelligence, a tool of immense potential, can revolutionize how we create and implement policies." Tonight, they would embark on a journey to understand how AI could transform their approach to governance and community development.

Their exploration began in the bustling city of Lusaka, where they visited the Zambian Institute of Technology. Here, they met with Dr. Mwape, a leading AI researcher. Amidst the hum of servers and the glow of computer screens, Dr. Mwape introduced them to the world of AI and its applications in policy making.

Chilufya and his team listened intently as Dr. Mwape explained how AI could analyze vast amounts of data to identify trends, predict outcomes, and optimize resource allocation. They learned about machine learning algorithms that could assist in decision-making processes, providing evidence-based recommendations and improving efficiency. The potential of AI to enhance transparency and accountability in governance was also highlighted.

Next, the team journeyed to the vibrant town of Livingstone, where they met with Ms. Kalaba, a policy advisor integrating AI into local government initiatives. In her modest office, Ms. Kalaba shared her experiences of using AI to address community challenges. She spoke of projects where AI analyzed data on public health, education, and infrastructure, leading to more effective and targeted interventions.

In Livingstone, Chilufya and his team witnessed firsthand the impact of AI on policy outcomes. They saw how AI could identify areas in need of urgent attention, predict the spread of diseases, and optimize public services. Ms. Kalaba emphasized the importance of ethical considerations and ensuring that AI systems were transparent, fair, and accountable.

Inspired by the insights from Lusaka and Livingstone, Chilufya and his team returned to Kasama with a renewed vision for the future. They convened a meeting under the baobab tree, inviting community leaders, residents, and technology experts to discuss the integration of AI into their policy-making processes.

Chilufya shared the lessons learned, emphasizing the transformative potential of AI in enhancing governance and community development. He spoke of the need for capacity building and digital literacy to ensure that the community could harness AI's benefits effectively. He highlighted the importance of ethical frameworks to guide the responsible use of AI and protect against biases and misuse.

One of the local teachers, Mr. Phiri, expressed his excitement about the potential of AI to improve educational outcomes. He spoke of how AI could provide personalized learning experiences for students and identify gaps in the education system. "By embracing AI, we can create a more inclusive and effective educational environment," he declared, "one that caters to the unique needs of every student."

The villagers nodded in agreement, their hearts filled with optimism. They spoke of creating a community where technology was leveraged to enhance the well-being of all residents. They acknowledged the role of each person in shaping the future of AI integration and pledged to work together to implement the strategies they had discussed.

The local councilors pledged their support, promising to prioritize investments in AI infrastructure and digital education. They agreed to work collaboratively with the community, ensuring that every step taken toward integrating AI into policy making was a step toward a more efficient, transparent, and equitable society.

As the stars cast their gentle glow over the village, Chilufya stood before the gathered multitude. "We have learned that in the realm of technology, we stand on the brink of a new era," he declared, his voice resonating with conviction. "Let us embrace the future with open hearts and minds, harnessing the power of AI to build a better, more just community for all."

With unity in their hearts and purpose in their steps, Chilufya and his team embraced the challenge of integrating AI into policy making, their resolve unyielding. They knew that the journey ahead would be complex, but their commitment to leveraging technology for the greater good would guide them every step of the way.

About the Author

Goodson Mumba is a multifaceted individual known for his diverse expertise and prolific contributions across various fields. As an infopreneur, Management Consultant, thought leader, and spiritual leader, he has inspired countless individuals through his insightful teachings and impactful writings. Mumba is also an accomplished author, with several notable works to his name, including "Understanding Corporate Worship," "The Years I Spent in a Week," "Management By Harmony," "The CEO's Diary," "Change to Change" and "Creative Thinking for results" His literary works span topics ranging from business management to personal development and spirituality, reflecting his broad range of interests and insights.

With a Master of Business Leadership (MBL) and a Bachelor of Arts in Theology (BTh), Mumba brings a unique blend of business acumen and spiritual wisdom to his work. His educational background is further enriched by a Group Diploma in Management Studies, providing him with a solid foundation in organizational dynamics and leadership principles. Additionally, Mumba holds diplomas in Education Psychology, Leadership and Management Styles, Organizational Behaviour, Financial Accounting, Economic Growth and Development, and Project Management, showcasing his commitment to continuous learning and professional development.

Mumba's expertise extends beyond traditional academic disciplines, encompassing areas such as Neuro-Linguistic Programming (NLP) and Positive Psychology. His diverse skill set is complemented by a range of certifications, including Creative Problem Solving and Decision Making, Life Coaching Fundamentals and Techniques, Professional Life Coaching, and Performance Management System Design. These certifications reflect Mumba's dedication to equipping himself with the tools and knowledge necessary to empower others and drive positive change.

As an author, Mumba's writings reflect his deep understanding of human nature, organizational dynamics, and spiritual principles. His works offer practical insights, actionable strategies, and inspirational guidance for individuals seeking personal growth, professional success, and spiritual fulfillment. Mumba's holistic approach to life and leadership resonates with readers worldwide, making him a respected figure in both the business and spiritual communities.

Overall, Goodson Mumba's diverse background, extensive knowledge, and profound insights make him a sought-after speaker, mentor, and author. His commitment to excellence, lifelong learning, and service to others continues to inspire individuals to unlock their full potential and lead lives of purpose and significance.

Goodson Mumba is renowned for initiating the concept

of Management by Harmony, revolutionizing traditional management practices with a focus on balanced and holistic approaches. He has authored two influential books on this subject: "Introduction to Management by Harmony" and its sequel, "Management by Harmony."

Mumba's work has significantly impacted the field, offering innovative strategies for fostering organizational harmony and efficiency. His contributions continue to shape contemporary management theories and practices.